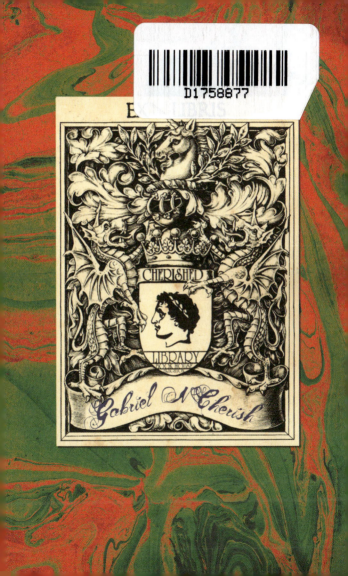

SCOTLAND
A Very Peculiar History

With NO added porridge
Volume 2

'God help England if she had no
Scots to think for her!'
George Bernard Shaw
(Irish dramatist, 1856–1950)

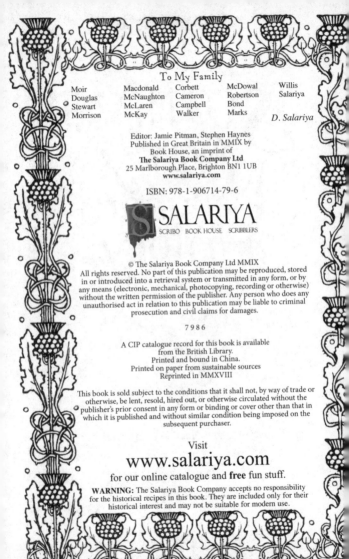

To My Family

Moir	Macdonald	Corbett	McDowal	Willis
Douglas	McNaughton	Cameron	Robertson	Salariya
Stewart	McLaren	Campbell	Bond	
Morrison	McKay	Walker	Marks	

D. Salariya

Editor: Jamie Pitman, Stephen Haynes
Published in Great Britain in MMIX by
Book House, an imprint of
The Salariya Book Company Ltd
25 Marlborough Place, Brighton BN1 1UB
www.salariya.com

ISBN: 978-1-906714-79-6

SALARIYA
SCRIBO   BOOK HOUSE   SCRIBBLERS

7 9 8 6

A CIP catalogue record for this book is available
from the British Library.
Printed and bound in China.
Printed on paper from sustainable sources
Reprinted in MMXVIII

Visit

www.salariya.com

for our online catalogue and **free fun stuff**.

WARNING: The Salariya Book Company accepts no responsibility
for the historical recipes in this book. They are included only for their
historical interest and may not be suitable for modern use.

SCOTLAND

A Very Peculiar History

Volume 2
From the Stewarts
to modern Scotland

With NO added porridge

fiona Macdonald

Created and designed by
David Salariya

Illustrated by
Mark Bergin

BOOK HOUSE
a SALARIYA imprint

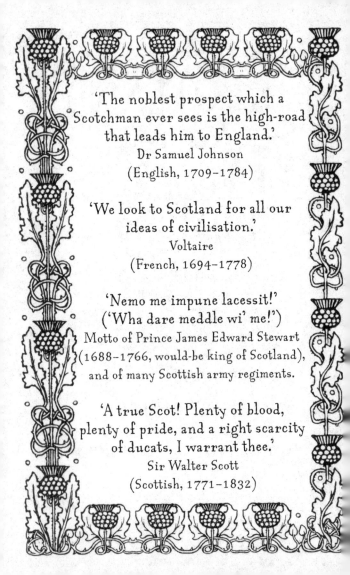

'The noblest prospect which a
Scotchman ever sees is the high-road
that leads him to England.'
Dr Samuel Johnson
(English, 1709–1784)

'We look to Scotland for all our
ideas of civilisation.'
Voltaire
(French, 1694–1778)

'Nemo me impune lacessit!'
('Wha dare meddle wi' me!')
Motto of Prince James Edward Stewart
(1688–1766, would-be king of Scotland),
and of many Scottish army regiments.

'A true Scot! Plenty of blood,
plenty of pride, and a right scarcity
of ducats, I warrant thee.'
Sir Walter Scott
(Scottish, 1771–1832)

Contents

of Volume 2

Ten Scottish firsts

1. **1617: First advanced calculating machine** 'Napier's Bones'– a set of ivory rods, engraved with figures, used to multiply and divide large numbers and to carry out more advanced calculations. Invented by mathematician Sir John Napier, who also invented logarithms.

2. **1712: First post office in Britain** Set up at Sanquhar, south-west Scotland, to handle messages carried across the English Border by couriers on horseback. Also said to be a meeting place for English and Scottish spies.

3. **1741: First public library** Founded by 21 miners, the schoolmaster and the minister at Leadhills, in the Borders. Each member paid a small entry fee and an annual subscription. The first books were mostly religious works.

4. **1780: First copying machine** Invented by engineer James Watt for making copies of business letters. He had the machine displayed in coffee-houses (where important men met) and demonstrated at the Houses of Parliament, the Bank of England and the royal court.

5. **1819: First works canteen** Set up by Robert Owen at his New Lanark Mills. He believed well-fed, healthy employees would work better.

6. **1824: First inflatable life jacket** Made by Charles MacIntosh (who also invented waterproof raincoats) for Sir John Franklin's Arctic expedition. Franklin took inflatable beds, as well. Like the life jackets, the coats were made of rubber-coated cotton, and were very, very smelly.

7. **1861: First colour photo** Taken by James Clerk Maxwell (1831–1879) and demonstrated to Britain's top scientists at the Royal Society in London. The photo showed a tartan ribbon.

8. **1872: First international football match** Played between teams from Scotland and England. Around 4,000 spectators watched the match, at Hamilton Crescent ground in Glasgow. The result? A draw: nil-nil.

9. **1887: First advertising film** Made to promote Haig's Scotch Whisky, this film is just one minute long. It shows a group of men in tartan kilts performing energetic Highland dancing.

10. **1908: First Boy Scout and Girl Guide groups** The 1st Glasgow Scout Troop and the Glasgow Girl Guide 'Cuckoo Patrol' were the first official groups of Scouts and Guides in Britain. Both were inspired by British army officer Robert Baden Powell's book *Scouting for Boys*, and by an earlier Scottish youth organisation, the Boys' Brigade (founded 1883).

Putting Scotland on the map

1. c.12,000 BC: Stone Age encampment at Biggar (see page 12)
2. c.3100 BC: Stone houses at Skara Brae
3. c.2500 BC: Stone circles at Brodgar and (3a) Callanish
4. c.1600 BC: Mummies at Cladh Hallan, South Uist
5. c 750 BC: Celtic hillfort at Eildon Hill
6. c.100 BC: Broch at Mousa
7. AD 84: Celts fight Romans at Mons Graupius
8. AD 122–143: Romans build Hadrian's Wall and (8a) Antonine Wall
9. AD 795–826: Vikings raid monastery on Iona
10. AD 842: Cinead MacAlpin crowned king at Scone
11. 1297 and 1314: Scots defeat English invaders at Stirling Bridge and Bannockburn
12. 1513: Scots badly defeated at battle of Flodden
13. 1557–1558: Religious riots after Protestant Reformer John Knox returns to Edinburgh
14. 1692: Massacre at Glencoe; MacDonald clan members killed by Campbells loyal to London
15. 1746: Hanoverians defeat Jacobites at Culloden
16. 1759: Carron Ironworks opens
17. c.1780–1820: Edinburgh New Town built
18. 1853: Queen Victoria starts to build Balmoral Castle
19. 1877–1890: Rail bridges over the Forth and (19a) Tay
20. 1882: Crofters fight landowners for rights to land
21. 2004: New Scottish Parliament building opens

Key to cities:

- Ⓐ Aberdeen
- Ⓓ Dundee
- Ⓔ Edinburgh
- Ⓖ Glasgow
- Ⓘ Inverness

Shetland Is.

Orkney Is.

HIGHLANDS

Outer Hebrides

Inner Hebrides

HIGHLANDS

LOWLANDS

LOWLANDS

ENGLAND

N. IRELAND

'These bagpipes have an irresistible rhythm,' said Farquhar, 'but I'm fair bamboozled by the steps!'

INTRODUCTION

This second and last volume of *Scotland: A Very Peculiar History* continues Scotland's story from 1371 until the early 21st century. It begins in turbulent times, when men die young (and mostly violently); it sighs over hopeless, romantic, Stewart rulers and rebels; and it sees Scotland lose its independence – but win international respect as the home of science and medicine and the 'workshop of the world'. Ancient Scottish traditions fade away – and are reinvented, mostly wrongly. Scots men and women spread their names, genes, energy, enterprise, hard work and intelligence all round the world, while, in return, millions of foreigners flock to Scotland as visitors or settlers. Scottish oil gushes, Scottish lochs go nuclear, Scottish glens glint with silicon, and Scottish pride rises with devolution.

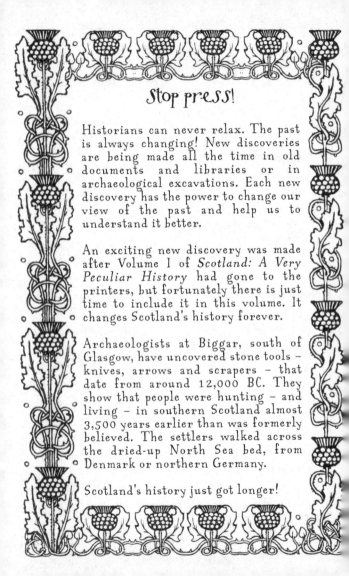

Stop press!

Historians can never relax. The past is always changing! New discoveries are being made all the time in old documents and libraries or in archaeological excavations. Each new discovery has the power to change our view of the past and help us to understand it better.

An exciting new discovery was made after Volume 1 of *Scotland: A Very Peculiar History* had gone to the printers, but fortunately there is just time to include it in this volume. It changes Scotland's history forever.

Archaeologists at Biggar, south of Glasgow, have uncovered stone tools – knives, arrows and scrapers – that date from around 12,000 BC. They show that people were hunting – and living – in southern Scotland almost 3,500 years earlier than was formerly believed. The settlers walked across the dried-up North Sea bed, from Denmark or northern Germany.

Scotland's history just got longer!

CHAPTER ONE

STEWART SCOTLAND

1371–1603

n 1371 King David II, the son of Robert the Bruce, dies without an heir, and his nephew Robert Stewart becomes King Robert II. New King Robert's mother was dead King David's sister, and his father was a senior royal official, the High Steward (said quickly, 'Steward' sounds like 'Stewart', and that's where King Robert's surname came from). Robert II founds a dynasty that rules Scotland until 1714 (and leaves at least 20 children, most of them illegitimate).

Stewart Scotland has some splendid highlights – and several very dark secrets. The early Stewart kings – and one queen! – all face similar problems...

It's tough at the top!
Stewart rulers must:

- Fend off threats from England
- Quash rival nobles and their private armies
- Strengthen the monarchy
- 'Civilise' their kingdom
- Control the Highlands
- Avoid becoming king too young – or too old!
- Stay alive!

1371

Amazingly – for a Scottish king – Robert II is not keen on war. His son (later Robert III) fights and rules for him. At first, Robert's son is traditionally strong and warlike, but in 1388 he is kicked by a horse. This leaves him lame and depressed. By the end of his life, he sobs: 'I am the worst of kings and most miserable of men.' And he wants to be buried in a dunghill!

In the north, nobles are in control. Some are very, very nasty. One of the worst is Robert III's brother, Alexander Stewart, known as Wolf of Badenoch. He attacks women, forces an heiress to marry him (to get a title and her family's land) and terrorises poor Highland farmers. He even loots and burns Elgin cathedral in 1390.

What a way to go!

Name & dates of reign	Age when crowned	Cause of death
Robert II 1371–1390	55	Old and 'feeble' (age 74)
Robert III 1390–1406	50	Depression, self-loathing
James I 1406–1437	13	Stabbed in a sewer
James II 1437–1460	6	Accident (exploding cannon)
James III 1460–1488	8	Knifed by assassin
James IV 1488–1513	15	Killed in battle
James V 1513–1542	1	Nervous breakdown
Mary 1542–1567	6 days	Beheaded
James VI 1567–1625	1	Old age (58!)

1383–1388

The Borders are not much better! In the middle of a truce, the English invade and attack Edinburgh. The Scots fight back and defeat the English, who are led by famous warrior Sir Henry Percy (known as Harry Hotspur), at the battle of Otterburn, in the Borderlands. A surprise Scottish success – although the Scottish commander (soon to be King Robert III) is seriously wounded.

Scotland's wild frontier

In spite of patrols by Scottish and English armies, the border between England and Scotland was still not fixed, and the Borderlands were home to gangs of wild, lawless Reivers (bandits and raiders). All Stewart kings fought against them. The most famous Reivers include Geordie Burn. When he was hanged in 1596, he boasted that he had 'killed seven Englishmen with his own hand' and 'spent his time whoring, drinking, stealing and taking deep revenge for slight offences'.

1396

The Highlands are just as lawless as the Borders. Royal power is weak, and there are constant feuds between ambitious chieftains and rival clans. At Perth, the Battle of the Clans displays Highland lawlessness as savage entertainment. While King Robert III looks on, two teams, each thirty men strong, from the clans MacIntosh and MacKay, fight for death or glory. Twenty wounded MacKays stagger off the 'playing' field, but only one MacIntosh survives.

1398

Did Henry St Clair, prince of Orkney, sail across the Atlantic like his Viking ancestors, to land in Nova Scotia? His family claims that he did, but most say this story is just a legend.

1402

Look, no heir! Robert III's jealous brother, the duke of Albany, has Robert's son locked away in a castle, where he dies, starved to death. It's said that the poor child gnawed at his own hands, desperate to eat anything.

Not quite the trip of a lifetime, more like the trip that lasts a lifetime! James is in the Tower of London for 18 years.

1406
Robert III sends his second son, James, to France for safety. The ship is attacked by pirates, and James is captured. It may be that Albany tipped them off. Young James is sold to the king of England, who has him locked in the Tower of London. When James's father, King Robert III, hears news of this, he collapses and dies of grief.

1411
The Battle of Harlaw: Highlands and Islands vs. Lowlands. Highland chiefs want to stay independent from Scottish kings, who are keen to control all Scotland. So much blood is spilt on each side that the contest is called 'Red Harlaw'. Both sides think they have lost, but later, both claim to have won.

The Highlanders at Harlaw are led by the MacDonald 'Lord of the Isles', who rules his own private kingdom from the isle of Islay. The Lords of the Isles have been a serious threat to Scottish kings since 1320. After six attempts, the last of them will be defeated by Stewart king James IV in 1494, and forced to spend the rest of his life in a monastery.

Highland life

- **What's a clan?** The (Gaelic) word originally meant 'children', but by the 1300s it meant families claiming descent from one long-dead ancestor, all loyal to their clan chief.

- **Where did clans live?** On lands in the Highlands owned, or claimed, by their chief. Land ownership was constantly challenged, and was decided by wars, murders and feuds.

- **How did clans survive?** By farming, fishing, hunting and gathering, as their ancestors had done since Iron Age times (see Volume 1).

- **What languages did Highlanders speak?** Gaelic in the north and west; Norse in the far north, Orkney and Shetland.

- **What did Highlanders wear?** Certainly not 'Highland dress' – short kilt, white socks, tight jacket – as worn by Scots for weddings and parties today. Most men wore a knee-length woollen tunic, and wrapped themselves in a *breacan* (long cloth about 5 metres by 2 metres). This may have been checked or striped, or various shades of fawn, cream, greenish-yellow or muddy blue (from natural wool or plant dyes). Women also wore the breacan, over a calf-length woollen tunic. Almost everyone went barefoot – and the men's rough, tanned bare legs earnt them the nickname of 'redshanks' from Lowlanders.

1413

In the middle of this mayhem, Scotland's first university is founded at St Andrews. Its aim is to protect the Scots from dangerous foreign ideas in religion and politics.

1424

After 18 years of imprisonment, James I is released by the English and begins to rule Scotland. He is keen to bring new, 'civilised', culture to Scotland. He rebuilds Linlithgow palace with a luxury interior. He encourages the writing of the *Scotichronicon* – a new national epic defining Scottish identity. It ends with the proud claim: 'Christ! He is not a Scot who is not proud of this book!'

James makes Scottish nobles and clan chiefs pay heavy taxes. If they refuse, he takes their land and castles away. For ordinary people, he bans rough sports (such as football) and fancy clothes. James also tries to ban late-night drinking – but fails.

1437

James I is murdered at Perth by angry nobles, unhappy with his government's reforms, and questioning his right to the throne. One loyal noblewoman, Kate Douglas, bars the door with her arm, but James's attackers fight their way in. They trap him in the castle sewer, like a rat, and stab him to death. Bad luck, Sire! If the sewer exit had not been blocked to stop balls from a nearby tennis court rolling in, you might have escaped and survived! James's wife gets her revenge by having the murderers horribly tortured – the executions last three days. James II is now king. Aged six, he is far too young to stop wars between ambitious rival nobles...

1440

For example, the Livingstone and Crichton families hold the 'Black Dinner' in Edinburgh castle. They invite the new young earl of Douglas and his brother (and heir), and serve a black bull's head to them. This is a well-known symbol of death, and they murder the Douglases after dinner, with James II, aged just 10, watching. A truly horrible evening!

The evening wasn't going to be remembered for the food or the company...

1449

James II is now old enough to rule. It's payback time for feuding nobles, especially those who have been plotting against the Stewarts. James murders another Earl of Douglas at Stirling Castle, in spite of having given him a promise of safe conduct for the meeting. More peacefully, James marries a fabulously rich heiress from the Burgundian royal family (Burgundy was an independent state – one of the richest in medieval Europe). And he has the first-known Scottish royal portrait painted – as a present for his sister.

1450

By now, Scottish towns and villages are beginning to recover from the Black Death. New trades and industries develop: fishing, salt-making, cloth-making – and mining. Foreigners are perplexed to observe Scots workers being paid with bags of black, shiny stones (coal).

But trade is hampered by royal taxes (to pay for wars, and royal luxuries such as new palaces and portraits). To try to make money go further, kings debase the Scottish coinage by mixing silver with base metals. By the end of the century, three Scottish mixed-silver coins equal one English pure silver one.

1457

James II and his nobles in the Edinburgh parliament try to ban football (again). For the first time, they also outlaw golf. They want Scottish men to prepare for war, instead, by practising shooting longbows before church every Sunday morning.

The Prentice Pillar

The famous Rosslyn Chapel, near Edinburgh, was built around 1460 by the last Prince of Orkney. All kinds of strange things are said to be shown in its carvings – including American plants, such as maize, long before Columbus crossed the Atlantic.

The chapel also contains the spectacular Prentice Pillar. This was carved by an apprentice after receiving instructions in a dream. His master was so jealous that he killed the apprentice... or so the legend says.

Golf: 'A Diversion Peculiar to Scotland'

- 'an unproffitable sport'
- 'a common and beloved amusement'
- 'a good walk spoiled'

Golf has been called all these things, and more. No-one knows where it originated, or when it was first played in Scotland. But by around 1600, the Scots themselves called it their own 'peculiar diversion' (special sport). A game that might have been the ancestor of golf (or hockey) was played in ancient Rome using wooden clubs and a leather ball stuffed with feathers. Around 1400, in the Netherlands, a similar game called *colf* (meaning 'club') was played on winter ice.

The first mention of golf in Scotland was in 1457, when King James II's parliament tried to ban it. They failed, and laws against golf were passed again in 1471 and 1490. But this royal disapproval soon disappeared and golf became a favourite sport of Scottish kings, queens and princes. James V, Mary Queen of Scots, James VI, Charles I, Charles II, James II and Bonnie Prince Charlie were all keen players.

Golf was also popular among all classes of Scottish people. They met to play on 'links' – stretches of dry, sandy land close to the sea – mostly on Sundays. This angered the Scottish Kirk (Church), which fined men and women golfers for 'breaking the Sabbath'. (The money was often used to buy refreshments for law-abiding church-goers.) Sometimes games ended in tragedy, for example in 1632, when 'ane deadlie straik' (one deadly stroke) from a golf ball killed a man in Kelso.

Scotland's first organised golf clubs were founded soon after 1700. The Royal Burgess Golfing Society, for ordinary citizens in Edinburgh, began in 1735, and the Honourable Company of Edinburgh Golfers, for gentlemen, in 1744. The Honorouble Company was the first to write down rules for the game. Then, in 1754, 22 'noblemen and gentlemen' organised a new competition open to all, at St Andrews. This was the beginning of the most famous golf tournament in the world, which is still played today.

Mary Queen of Scots enjoys a round of golf.

1460

James II is killed – by his own cannon! It explodes while he is showing it off to his wife, at the siege of Roxburgh castle, which is being held by the English. After James dies, she continues with the siege, which is successful. She also builds a new castle, Ravenscraig. Wisely, it's designed to be cannon-proof.

1469

The next king, James III, marries Margaret, the daughter of the king of Denmark. She brings Orkney and Shetland as marriage gifts. Scotland is now as big as it will ever be. It stretches from the lawless southern borderlands to the northernmost Shetland isle.

1482

James III increases taxes, interferes with law-courts – and has his younger brothers tried for witchcraft! It's one sure-fire way of getting rid of enemies, especially ones plotting against you. Scottish nobles decide he must go. They seize his closest advisers and friends, and hang them from a bridge. Helpless and horrified, James is forced to look on.

Wedding gifts

SHETLAND

ORKNEY

'We mustn't forget to thank your parents for the islands.'

1488
James III fights the nobles, and loses, at the battle of Sauchieburn. It's said that, as James shelters in a peasant hovel, he is murdered by a mysterious stranger – on the orders of his son!

New king James IV wears a heavy iron chain round his waist as penance for having his father murdered. But this doesn't hold him back. These are exciting times and James is interested in all the latest ideas: exploration, art and architecture, science and technology, poetry, new learning…

James sets up a glittering court and makes Edinburgh the capital of Scotland. He begins to build a new palace, at Holyrood. He pays poets to live there, and holds famous *flytings* (slanging matches) between them.

1493
James wants to find out where words come from. So he sends a woman who is deaf and cannot speak to live alone on Inchkeith island with two babies, to see whether they will grow up to speak, and, if so, what language they will use. Royal chroniclers, trained by the Church, claim that they spoke Hebrew.

Scots speak Scots

Perhaps James IV's curiosity is inspired by the fact that a new language is becoming widespread in Lowland Scotland. It is even used by his royal officials to write government documents. Confusingly called *Inglis*, it is based on Anglo-Saxon, with Gaelic, Norse, Dutch and French words mixed in. Today, we call it 'Scots'. Scots grammar is quite like English, but many things have different names.

Many Anglo-Saxon words are pronounced differently north of the Border. For example: heid = head; coo = cow; gude or guid = good; ane = one; twa or twae = two; fou = full; gowd = gold.

Can you translate this Scots story?

Ane dreich nicht, the douce wee lassie gaed oot frae her hame in the vennel and doun the kirk brae tae the braw loch in the bonnie glen. She was heading for a ceilidh in the manse and carried an ashet with a gigot, a jeely piece, and a poke o' bawbees. She crossed the brig over the muckle burn, and spied a peely-wally callant by the midden next tae the fank. He was wearing breeks, brogues and a bunnet, holding a futba, and greeting. 'Dinnae fash yersel the noo,' she crooned. 'I'm fair wabbit! I've a sair lug', he replied. 'And yon crabbit dominie gied me a dunt on the broo.'

(translation on page 52)

1503

In a bid to end wars with England, James IV marries the daughter of English king Henry VII. He had been in love with his Scottish sweetheart, Margaret Drummond. But, most suspiciously, she and her two sisters die from poisoning!

1506

The Royal College of Surgeons is founded in Edinburgh. James likes to practise dentistry – on prisoners. To encourage further learning, and tame over-mighty nobles, James orders all the most important families in Scotland to send their sons to school.

1507

Scotland's first printing press is set up in Edinburgh.

1511

James IV builds a new navy, and a splendid new warship. The *Great Michael* is the biggest ship in Europe – around twice the size of the *Mary Rose*, flagship of English king Henry VIII. It is said that all the trees in Fife (a rich royal region) have been cut down to provide the timber.

The 'Birdman of Stirling' plummets into history

Who? Italian alchemist, John Damian de Falcuis, promised James IV he could turn base metal into gold, and claimed that he could fly. In 1507 he made wings from wood and chicken feathers and jumped from the walls of Stirling Castle. Luckily, he survived, landing in the castle dungheap with a broken leg. He blamed the feathers for his failure, saying that they had 'drawn him' to the dung, which no doubt included dirty straw from the castle henhouses.

A swoop into the poop!

Home and away

From around 1400, thousands of Scots moved to live in the Netherlands, Poland, Scandinavia, Ireland, Russia and, of course, France. They worked as soldiers, scholars, sailors, fishermen – and pirates.

Scots traders sold wool, salt, coal, hides, malt, tallow (sheep's fat, used for candles) and salmon.

Today, many families – especially in Poland – still have names such as Ramzy ('Ramsay' in Scottish), showing that they are descended from Scots settlers.

Meanwhile, people from northern Europe also moved to settle in Scotland. Legends claim that John O'Groats, the northernmost settlement on the Scottish mainland, is named after a 15th-century Dutch ferryman, Jan de Groot.

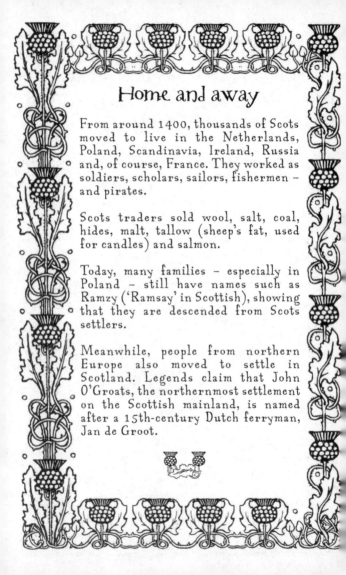

1513

The 'Flowers of the Forest' fade away. Eleven earls, fifteen lords, two abbots, James's illegitimate son (an archbishop), hundreds of knights, thousands of foot-soldiers and King James himself are killed fighting the English, on the side of France, at the Battle of Flodden, in Northumberland. It's Scotland's worst defeat and a military disaster.

James's death heralds the arrival of another baby king: James V. His widowed mother marries a member of the hated Douglas family, who puts James in prison. James escapes, aged 16, and later gets his revenge on the Douglas family by having Janet Douglas, Lady Glamis burnt as a witch.

1537–1538

James V turns to France for help (with running the country, fighting England and producing an heir) – and becomes the only Scots king to marry two French brides in under two years. The first one dies – she can't stand the Scottish cold.

The flowers of the forest

One of the most famous poems in Scotland – but probably also one of the least read today. It is written in a polite, old-fashioned, literary version of Scots which even most Scottish people now find hard to understand.

'The Flowers of the Forest' was composed in 1776 in memory of the Scottish soldiers who died at the Battle of Flodden. Its author was Jane Elliott (1727–1805), the daughter of a leading Scottish lawyer. Her words look back, nostalgically and romantically, imagining country life in 1513.

I've heard the lilting at our yowe-milking,
Lasses a-lilting before the dawn of day;
But now they are moaning in ilka green
    loaning:
'The Flowers of the Forest are a' wede away.'

[lilting = singing; yowe = ewe (female sheep); ilka = each; loaning = lane; a' = all; wede = withered]

At buchts, in the morning, nae blythe lads are
    scorning;
The lasses are lonely, and dowie, and wae.
Nae daffin, nae gabbin, but sighing and sabbing:
Ilk ane lifts her leglen and hies her away.

[buchts = sheepfolds; nae = no; blythe = cheerful; scorning = teasing; lasses = girls; dowie = sad; wae = woeful; daffing = playing; gabbing = chatter; sabbing = sobbing; Ilk … hies her away = Each girl picks up her milk-pail and wanders away]

Battle of Flodden, 1513

1539

James V has big ideas about royal power, and wants a shiny new symbol to display them. He orders a golden imperial dome-shaped crown. It shows that he is the sole ruler in his kingdom – or at least claims to be. James owns another symbol of Scots kingship: a real live lion, which is kept in his castle at Stirling.

The nobles hate James V, because he is trying to keep them under control, but he's popular with the ordinary folk. He likes to disguise himself as the 'Gudeman of Ballengeich' and wander through the streets, chatting to them.

1542

Another invasion of England – against the advice of the Scots army, who don't value James's judgement. The Scots are defeated and James takes to his bed, weak with disease. A week later, he hears that his wife has given birth to a girl – his only heir. He mutters, 'It cam wi' ane lass and will gang wi' ane lass!',[1] turns his face to the wall, and dies.

---

1 Stewart power came with a girl (Robert the Bruce's daughter, who was the mother of Robert II) and will go out with a girl.

1542

Crowned at the age of just six days, and female too! Mary Queen of Scots causes problems from the start. She grows up to be beautiful, brave, wilful, tragic – a victim, a heroine, a martyr and a fool!

1544

The 'Rough Wooing' begins. Henry VIII of England wants Scotland. He hopes to get it by marrrying baby Mary to his own infant son. He sends armies to 'persuade' the Scots, but, understandably, they will not accept his proposal.

1548

For safety, Mary Queen of Scots, aged 6, is sent to France. At the age of 15, she is married to the French crown prince, and becomes Queen of France a year later. A secret clause in her marriage treaty joins Scotland to France. By 18 she's a widow, and no longer welcome at the French court. But she still thinks and dreams in French, and spells her royal name 'Stuart', in the French way.

1560

'The most important year in Scots history' – or so religious reformers say. The Scottish Parliament votes to make Scotland a Protestant nation. Scots Protestants reject the authority of the Pope in Rome, and disagree with the Roman Catholic Church over the meaning of important Christian rituals. They want simple ways of worshipping, plus the right to run their own churches and choose their own ministers (religious leaders).

1561

Bonjour, Madame la Reine! Mary Queen of Scots arrives back in Scotland. Protestants demonstrate against her Catholic faith the moment she sets foot in Edinburgh. The rioters include actors dressed as characters from the Bible, warning what happens to 'unholy' rulers.

In private meetings, Protestant preacher John Knox thunders at Mary and reduces her to tears – mostly of exasperation. Mary feels alone and afraid.

Reformation Scotland

This is a time of bitter religious wars across Europe, but, so far, 'barbaric' Scotland has escaped without too much bloodshed. There have, of course, been a few little local difficulties:

- In 1546, Protestant preacher George Wishart is burned at the stake in St Andrews.

- In retaliation, Catholic Cardinal Beaton is murdered, and his naked body is hung from his own castle walls.

- The Cardinal's Protestant murderers and their supporters are captured by Catholic troops from France.

- Captives include Protestant preacher John Knox, who is sent to be a galley slave.

- Eventually freed, Knox returns to Scotland. His preaching stirs up strong religious feelings on all sides. After one rousing sermon, an Edinburgh Protestant mob snatches the holy statue of St Giles as it is being carried in a Catholic festival procession – and throws it in the river!

- Soon, angry Protestants in many towns are looting and smashing church treasures in a frenzy of hatred for what they call 'idols'.

'No more tears now:
I will think on
revenge.'

Mary Queen of Scots,
after the murder of David Rizzio.

1565

Mary meets Henry, Lord Darnley on Valentine's Day. Is he of noble rank? Yes! Tall, dark and handsome? Yes! A good fighter? Yes! But he's NOT the ideal husband! Darnley's weak, silly, power-mad, drunken, extravagant, sulky, violent, diseased, and given to roaming the streets at night. Even so, Mary marries him – and spends her honeymoon in tears.

1566

Sometimes, having a good voice can be dangerous. Italian David Rizzio is recruited to Mary's household because she needs a deep-voiced singer. Mary already has three singing servants and wants a quartet to entertain her. Rizzio works as her secretary – and soon Darnley becomes very jealous. He sends friends to Mary's rooms with daggers. They have murder on their minds. Rizzio is stabbed to death (56 times!) – but was Mary herself the real target?

Three months later, Mary has Darnley's baby – a son! Hooray! Scotland has a new heir.

1567

Darnley falls ill, and Mary nurses him. But, on one particular night, she goes to stay elsewhere. That very evening, Darnley's house explodes, leaving Darnley's lifeless corpse in the garden. But he's been strangled, not blown up! Who killed him? Does Mary know? Yes, probably...

Already, she's in love with another unsuitable man: James Hepburn, Earl of Bothwell, a rough, uncouth bully. He's violent – even murderous – and has left a trail of deserted women behind him.

Bothwell kidnaps Mary – and marries her at 4.00a.m.! Does he force her (as she claims) or, more likely, is Mary already pregnant with his twins? The Scots nobles are shocked. They lock Mary up in a castle, where her unborn babies die, and insist that she can no longer be queen.

Bothwell flees to Denmark, where he is captured, chained to a pillar and goes mad. Sixteenth-century tourists pay to gawp at him.

Mary's son, James VI, becomes king at just 13 months old. There are nine attempts to kidnap him. Fearing daggers and swords, he wears padded clothes all the time. Being a Scottish king is no picnic!

1581

It's also risky being regent (royal guardian and governor). After a quarrel with the teenage James, the earl of Morton, regent since 1572, is arrested and beheaded for treason. He's killed by a deadly invention, only recently introduced to Scotland – the Maiden (guillotine).

1585

James VI takes control of Scotland – and governs well, on the whole. His 40-year rule, to 1625, is welcomed as 'King James's Peace'.

But as James grows up, it's clear that he lacks Mary's grace, charm and beauty. He's cautious, thoughtful, studious – he speaks Latin before he learns Scots! But at the same time he's gruff, clumsy, shabby and covered in mud (he loves hunting). People call him 'the Wisest Fool in Christendom'.

1587

Mary Queen of Scots is executed, in England, for plotting against English queen Elizabeth I. For her beheading, Mary wears blood-red robes, with a lap-dog under her skirts so that her dead body goes on 'moving'. When the axeman picks up her severed head, it falls from his horrified hands – that's her wig he's left holding!

1589

James VI marries Princess Anne of Denmark. James has had many close friendships with handsome young men. But he likes Anne, too, and they have seven children.

The ideal wedding present...

...is a hen! That's the Scottish tradition. You should give it to the bride's mother, to cook and serve to her guests as part of the wedding feast. She'll have a party in the kitchen too, as she cooks with her female friends and helpers – the original hen party! Other Scottish courtship and wedding traditions include:

- **Bundling** Get into bed with your boyfriend or girlfriend, but fully dressed and with your legs bound together. That way, you can spend all night cuddling – but nothing more!

- **Handfasting (trial wedding)** Make a public promise to be true to your loved one, and live with them for a year as if you were married. After that, you can marry (especially if there is a baby on the way) or part in a friendly, honourable way.

- **Reitach ('Ree-taahh' – Gaelic betrothal)** Go to your girlfriend's house and ask her father for permission to marry. If he agrees, you and your girlfriend must drink whisky from a special bridal cup together. Now you're engaged. It's official!

- **Wear a wedding ring** – not a gold band, but a ring shaped like clasped hands – on your right thumb or ring finger.

- **Wait for a new moon** to hold the wedding ceremony – but never marry in May. It's sacred to the Virgin Mary.

James sails to Denmark to meet his bride and escort her to Scotland. The weather is foul, and on the way back they are nearly shipwrecked. James blames witches, and witch trials are held at North Berwick near Edinburgh. Women there are accused of 'roasting' wax images of James VI, 'to the undoing of the king's person', and of casting a bewitched cat into the sea, to cause storms and wreck ships. The cat swims home safely again, but the witches suffer far worse fates. These sensational trials, and others like them, whip up public hysteria.

1593

King James writes *Daemonologie*, all about witches. For centuries, witches have claimed to harm or heal, and many Scots have believed them. But now religious reformers think that witchcraft is something new and deeply sinister: devil worship! They claim that witches curse people, kill people, destroy crops, wreck bridges and eat babies.

Witchcraft has been banned in Scotland since 1563, and 'witch-prickers' travel round the Lowlands, hunting witches for execution.

They stick pins into suspects (if they don't bleed, they are guilty) or 'wake' them (stop them sleeping for three days and nights, so that they become confused, and 'confess').

c.1600
More wreckers! It's claimed that Sawney (Alexander) Bean and his family grow rich by wrecking ships off Ballantrae on the west coast of Scotland. They murder the survivors, steal their goods, and eat the dead bodies! There are rumours of a frightful cave on the seashore, full of stolen treasures – and barrels of pickled human remains!

It's a chilling tale, but historians can find no trace of Sawney Bean or his family in any ancient documents. Sawney's story first appears in print about 100 years after he was said to have lived so murderously. Some historians think it was invented by the English at the time of the Jacobite rebellions (see page 70), to smear the Scots and portray them as savages. Others think it is a genuine folktale, which preserves the memory of past famines when starving people really did eat dead bodies out of desperation.

The end of Highland culture?

James VI is badly bothered by independent-minded Highland chiefs, as well as by witches. Throughout his reign, he takes stern steps to get rid of ancient Highland traditions. He thinks this will be the best way to end the Highlanders' power.

1597
James leases the Isle of Lewis to the 'Fife Adventurers' – a group of Lowland nobles and soldiers led by his cousin, the Duke of Lennox. Lewis is the largest island in the Outer Hebrides, and a stronghold of Gaelic language and tradition. The Adventurers are instructed to 'root out the barbarian inhabitants' by fire and the sword.

1609
James tricks top Highland chieftains into boarding a Scottish navy ship. The Highlanders are marooned on the tiny island of Iona in the Hebrides, and only released when they agree to obey tough new laws:

- All Highlanders must have a proper job (rather than fighting for a chief).
- Clan chiefs must have just one home (so James's soldiers know where to find them).
- Chiefs cannot keep as many armed followers as they used to.
- Chiefs may not import too much French wine.

- Inns must be built to shelter royal messengers – and spies – in the Highlands.
- Guns are banned, even for hunting.
- Chiefs' ships must be small.
- Bards – Gaelic poets who praise chiefs and preserve traditions – are banned.
- Chiefs' sons must learn to read and write (in English), or they cannot inherit clan lands.
- Chiefs and leading Highlanders must attend James's royal court once a year.
- Chiefs are responsible for all the actions of all their clansmen.
- Handfasting (traditional trial marriage) is banned.

fire and sword

Clan MacLeod of the isle of Skye and clan MacDonald of the isle of Eigg have been enemies for centuries. In 1577, the MacLeods raided Eigg. They herded the whole population – 395 men, women and children – into a cave, lit a bonfire outside, and suffocated the lot.

In 1578, MacDonalds from another island, Uist, took revenge. They surrounded the church on Skye where dozens of MacLeod clansfolk were praying, and set fire to it. Only one little girl escaped alive, by squeezing through a window. She raised the alarm, and the rest of the MacLeods chased the MacDonalds back to their boats. The tide was out. They were stranded, trapped – and killed.

1600

James VI is kidnapped – or pretends to be – by the earl of Gowrie. He wants the Gowrie castle and lands, but, by law, these can only go to him if Gowrie is found guilty of treason. Gowrie's already dead – he was killed when James was freed from his kidnappers. So he's dug up, put on trial – and convicted!

1603

Gowrie's not the only dead man to appear in court. Francis Moubray, a prisoner in Edinburgh Castle, escapes from his cell by tying sheets together and climbing out of the window. He falls and dies, but is still put on trial. Found guilty, his body is hung, drawn and quartered; his head and body parts are then displayed on the gates guarding the city.

Translation of the story on page 51

One damp, dreary night, the sweet little girl went out of her home in the narrow lane and down the church hill to the fine lake in the beautiful valley. She was heading for a party in the minister's house and carried an oven-slab with a leg of lamb, a jam sandwich, and a little bag of pennies. She crossed the bridge over the big stream and saw a pale and feeble-looking young boy by the rubbish heap next to the sheepfold. He was wearing long trousers, laced-up shoes and a cap, was holding a football and was crying. 'Don't upset yourself now,' she said gently, 'I'm tired out! My ear hurts!' he replied. 'And that bad-tempered teacher thumped me on the head!'

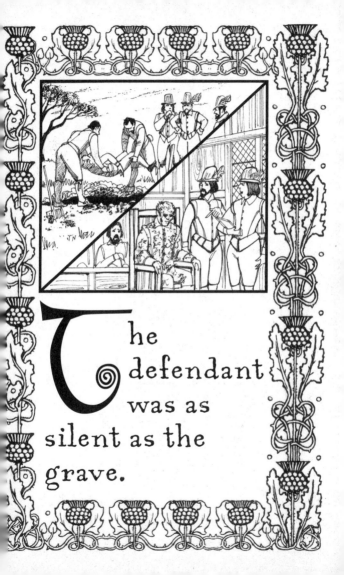

The defendant was as silent as the grave.

Witchcraft and smoking really scunnered* James VI.

disgusted

CHAPTER TWO

UNITED KINGDOMS?

1603–1746

From 1603, for the first time ever, Scotland and England have the same ruler, although they remain separate kingdoms, each with its own parliament. Scotland also keeps its own army, navy, national church, coins, weights and measures, schools, languages (Scots and Gaelic) and laws. But how long can Scotland stay independent from its stronger, richer neighbour?

'Has He [God] not made us all one island, compassed [surrounded] with one sea and of itself by nature indivisible [unable to be divided]?'

James VI, in a speech to the English Parliament

1603

King twice over! James VI of Scotland becomes King James I of England. He is now known as 'James VI and I'. Queen Elizabeth I of England has died without any children, and James VI, her cousin, is her closest heir. James leaves Scotland for England, and rules Scotland (as he himself says) 'by the pen'. That is, he sends written instructions from London to his government ministers in Edinburgh.

1604

A new book by King James reveals his pet hate: smoking! Tobacco has only recently arrived in Scotland from North America. James calls smoking: 'A custome loathesome to the eye, hateful to the nose, harmful to the brain, dangerous to the lungs...'

1605

James nearly vanishes in an enormous cloud of smoke – and flames – when Guy Fawkes and his fellow conspirators plot to blow up the London Parliament while James is making a speech there. This 'Gunpowder Plot' is a protest by English Catholics against anti-Catholic laws passed by the English parliament while England is fighting Catholic Spain. The plot is foiled with only hours to spare, and the conspirators are tried and executed.

1608
James makes a tragic mistake. He sends Scottish Protestants to settle in Ireland, to subdue Catholic rebels. By 1650, over 50,000 Scots have moved to live there. This leads to centuries of bitterness and fighting between Protestants and Catholics.

1611
James sponsors a brilliant new translation of the Bible into English. It is widely used by Protestants throughout Scotland, weakening the use of Gaelic. The King James Bible, also known as the Authorised Version, is still used in much of the English-speaking world today.

1616
The Kirk (Church of Scotland) sets up schools in every parish in Scotland to teach 'goodness and knowledge'. Lessons are held in English. The Kirk claims that Gaelic is 'the chief cause of the barbaritie and incivilitie of the people'.

The Lowlands: 'rude neglect'

In 1619, English travel writer Fynes Moryson reports on Lowland Scottish lifestyle for curious English readers. What catches his eye?

- **Food:** too much cabbage, too little meat; oatcakes, not bread; no fancy tableware, a 'rude neglect' of furnishings – and an awful lot of porridge!

- **Beds in cupboards** (alcoves with doors) – and sheet sleeping bags!

- **Clothes:** woollen tunics and trousers (for men) and long dresses (for women), made from homespun wool and 'sky blue'. (Alas, given the Scottish weather, this means blue-grey.) Women also wear white linen 'toys' (headscarves), but men sport big blue woollen bonnets (like berets) made using the latest technology – knitting! Plaid cloaks (with coloured checks) are popular with both men and women.

Other travellers complain that in some Scottish houses the cobwebs are as thick as blankets, and that the streets of Edinburgh 'stink of haddock and skate' (a fish that smells of ammonia).

The Highlands: 'smoking dunghills'

In the Highlands, poor farm cottages are dark, stuffy, sooty, and often half-full of manure: Highlanders keep their cows indoors during the winter. English visitors call them 'smoking dunghills'.

Canny Highlanders sit on low 'cutty (short-legged) stools', below the smoke swirling up to the rafters. But guests are offered the 'high seat', often the only normal-sized chair in the house – an honour, but not a very pleasant one!

1621

Some Scots opt for a new life overseas. Settlers found the first Scottish colony in the Americas, Nova Scotia (New Scotland), now part of Canada. It fails. But Scots are still in demand as soldiers, especially in France, Poland and Russia. Scotsmen Patrick Gordon and James Keith both command Russian armies; Samuel Keith is admiral of a Russian fleet. Many more Scots will follow them.

1625–1633

James VI and I dies peacefully of old age and his son, Charles I, becomes king. But Charles gets off to a bad start. He waits eight years before he visits Scotland to be crowned. The Scots feel neglected and insulted, and Scottish nobles are angry when Charles tries to make them pay to support an English-style Church in Scotland. At last, Charles heads north. He wants to meet the top Scots in a fine new Parliament House in Edinburgh, but the cost is phenomenal. The Scots protest at the extravagance of the Parliament building – just as they will again in the early 2000s, almost 400 years later.

1637

Mind your head! Charles I also wants to change the Scottish Protestant Church; he thinks its beliefs are too extreme. Scots Protestants – the majority of Scottish men and women – want no bishops, no elaborate services, and no decorations inside church buildings. Outraged Protestant women throw their seats at the new preacher sent by Charles to St Giles' Cathedral, Edinburgh.

Edinburgh Protestants object to the new-style church service.

8cotswomen certainly know how to fling the furniture.

> 'In religion there is no middle.'
>
> John Knox

1638

Fervent Scots Protestants draw up a petition in protest against Charles, called the National Covenant. To show that they're deadly serious, many 'Covenanters' (as they are called) sign it in blood!

1642–1649

Civil War. South of the border, in England, Charles is at war with the English Parliament. (Charles believes he has a 'Divine Right' to rule. But Parliament insists that it must be consulted about new laws and new taxes.) Charles is captured by Parliament's army. He promises religious freedom to the Scots, if they will help him. The Scots agree but are defeated by the English Parliament's army at Preston, England, in 1648. The next year, Charles is executed in London.

1650

English Parliament troops, led by Lord Protector Oliver Cromwell, invade Scotland. Until 1660, Scotland is occupied by a foreign (English) army – for the first and only time in its history.

The Honours of Scotland

In 1652, Cromwell demanded that the Honours of Scotland be sent to London. These are Scotland's symbols of nationhood: a royal crown, sword and sceptre. The Scots hid them in remote, clifftop Dunottar Castle for eight months, then dropped them secretly over the castle walls. They were collected from the beach below by a trusty maid pretending to gather seaweed. She took them to the local minister and his wife, who hid them under the floor of their church for safety. In 1660, when the fighting was over, the Honours were taken to Edinburgh castle, and displayed at meetings of the Scottish Parliament. From 1707, they were locked away in a secret cupboard – and forgotten! – until they were rediscovered in 1818.

The Honours leave Dunottar Castle, disguised as baskets of seaweed.

1651

New king Charles II (son of Charles I) is crowned King of the Scots at Scone – where he is hiding from the English Parliament – before escaping overseas to France. He never returns to Scotland, and is the last king to be crowned on Scottish soil.

1655

Parliamentary armies build the first English fort in Scotland – Maryburgh, also known as Fort William – to control the Highlands.

1660

Parliament's rule ends, and Charles II returns to England. He's welcomed there, but is much less popular with Protestants in Scotland – most of the population – because he tries to tell them how their Church should be run.

Angry Covenanters (see page 62) go into hiding, and hold secret prayer meetings. Their leaders wear masks and wigs so that no-one will recognise them.

1666

The Pentland Rising. Rebel Covenanters are defeated at the battle of Rullion, near Edinburgh, by King Charles's Scottish general, Sir Tam Dalziel. The captives are shipped to Barbados in the West Indies.

In the same year, the baillies (leading men) of Edinburgh drive beggars and homeless people 'not fit to stay in the kingdom' out of their city. They transport them to Virginia, North America, to be sold as indentured (unfree) labourers, or as slaves.

Dalziel ('Dee~ELL') and the Devil ('DEE~ell')

Sir Tam Dalziel was a stern, proud, professional soldier. Legend tells how he once played cards with the Devil – and won! The Devil was so angry that he picked up the heavy stone table where they had been sitting, and threw it into the lake outside Dalziel's great house. It was found 200 years later, when the lake was emptied. The cards and drinking glasses used during the game survived – so did Dalyell's great riding boots. But they all vanish when Dalziel's ghost appears, and wanders round the house and gardens.

1678

The Highland Host. No, this is not a welcome for tourists. Ruffianly Highland soldiers are sent to terrorise Covenanters by staying in – and trashing – their homes. In return, Covenanters ambush and murder Charles's senior churchman in Scotland, the Archbishop of St Andrews, in 1679.

1681–1685

The 'Killing Time'. Around 100 rebel Covenanters are killed by Charles II's troops. They include the Wigtown Martyrs: two women tied to a post on the beach and left to drown as the tide rolls in. Other Covenanters are shot without trial, or tortured using terrible 'pain machines': thumbscrews (that crush the victim's fingers) and 'the boot' (that shatters legs).

1685–1689

Charles II dies, and a new king of Scotland and England, James VII and II, is crowned. Charles II's younger brother, and a Catholic, James is described by a friend as: 'a brave and honest man, but the silliest I have ever seen in my life.'

The voice of the Lord is upon the waters.

Psalm 29

Wigtown Martyrs Margaret Wilson (18) and Margaret McLauchlan (63)

1688

James's queen gives birth to a son and heir. Well, that's what his supporters say. The news is celebrated, by royal command, with feasting and bonfires, but all the queen's previous babies have died, and she is past the usual age for child-bearing.[1] It's whispered that this baby – James Edward – has been smuggled into the queen's room in a warming pan.[2]

Waaah!

1   The queen is James's second wife; he has two grown-up daughters, Mary and Anne. Their mother, now dead, was his mistress, whom he later married.

2   This rumour led to a rather strange British custom: by law, until the mid-20th century, all royal births had to be attended by the Home Secretary (Minister for Justice), as well as by doctors and midwives! With such an important witness to each birth, there should be no more disputed royal offspring.

   The last royal baby to be born in the presence of the Home Secretary was Princess Margaret (sister of Queen Elizabeth II), at Glamis Castle in Scotland in 1930. Then, the Home Secretary was a senior Labour Party politician, who began his campaigning career as organiser for the Lancashire Gasworkers' Union!

1688

The 'Glorious Revolution'. King James demands changes to the law, mostly to help Catholics. The English are outraged. This is a threat to their Parliament's independence! English MPs and army commanders plot to get rid of James. They invite his daughter Mary to rule instead, together with her husband, the Dutch Protestant prince William of Orange. Fearing for their lives, King James, his queen and their new baby flee to France, then Rome. Soon afterwards, in 1689, the Scottish Parliament declares that James has 'forfeited the Scottish crown'.

1689–1702

Ministers do the Scottish shuttle. William and Mary become king and queen of both Scotland and England, but neither ever sets foot in Scotland. Their Scots government ministers travel between the Scottish Parliament in Edinburgh and the royal court in London. They use the most up-to-date transport for this 'shuttle diplomacy': horse-drawn stage-coaches. The journey now takes less than a week. How speedy!

1689

The Scottish Protestant Church and the Scottish Parliament welcome William and Mary. So do many Lowlanders. But Scots Catholics, mostly from the Highlands, and some Scots Protestants, are not happy. They believe that James VII – the senior living member of the Stewart royal family – is their rightful king, and will protect their chosen ways of worshipping. They become known as 'Jacobites' (after *Jacobus*, the Latin version of 'James').

Led by handsome, dashing Lord Claverhouse, Viscount Dundee (nicknamed 'Bonnie Dundee' by his friends, but 'Bloody Clavers' by his enemies), the Jacobites fight a Scottish Parliament army at Killiecrankie in Perthshire. But Claverhouse is killed, and their rebellion collapses.

Killiecrankie leaves a very bitter legacy. For the next 50 years and more, Scottish people are divided – and the English government is scared.

Dressed to kill

Claverhouse was killed by gunshot – some say he received warning in a ghostly premonition. By now, many of King William's troops and Scots Parliament soldiers are armed with hand-guns, but Highlanders still fight with their traditional weapons: claymore (long sword), dirk (dagger) and the fearsome Lochaber axe (a spiked blade on a long pole). Their preferred battle-tactic is a surprise, headlong charge down a steep hill.

Highland dress is well suited to this style of fighting. Men wear hose – tubes of 'Tirtaine' (a French word meaning thin woollen cloth, which in Scotland was often striped or checked) covering their lower legs – and tough laced shoes made of a single piece of leather. They wear a long, saffron-yellow linen shirt, which can be knotted between the legs to give freedom of movement. To this they add a linen neckerchief, a sleeveless woollen jerkin, a thick, fringed *plaid* (a length of cloth wrapped round the body), and a blue knitted bonnet.

No kilts – and no trousers!

1690–1700

Scotland is starving. Climate change – the 'Little Ice Age' – leads to seven poor harvests, one after the other. People run short of food; about one in ten Scots dies from starvation. Poor Scottish families sell some of their children as indentured labourers (unfree workers, like slaves) to owners of tobacco plantations in America, in order to get money to pay for provisions.

1692

Slaughter in the snow. As a test of support for King William and Queen Mary, Highland chiefs are asked to swear an oath of loyalty. One chief, MacDonald of Glencoe, is just a few days late in doing so. It's appalling January weather – even today, Glencoe can get cut off in winter – and he's been deliberately told, by King William's government officials, to go to the wrong office.

It's a plot! The MacDonalds have been accused of supporting the Jacobites, and so Scottish nobles working for William have decided to teach them a lesson. Royal official the Master of Stair sends 120 troops to stay in Glencoe. They are led by Campbell of Glenlyon; for centuries, Campbells and MacDonalds have been enemies. As Highland custom demands, the MacDonalds feed and shelter the troops for almost two weeks. Then, one cold morning at 5.00a.m., the soldiers drive the MacDonalds out into the snow, shooting the chief and 37 clansmen. They strip the chief's wife of her clothes and gnaw the rings off her fingers. She dies, naked and frozen.

1695

The Bank of Scotland is founded – and Scots invent overdrafts! Known as the 'Old Bank', the Bank of Scotland is the first national bank to operate in Scotland. The Bank of Scotland is joined by the 'New Bank' (the Royal Bank of Scotland) in 1727. Together, they pioneer many new ways of handling money, such as:

• Widespread use of paper money, in the form of banknotes
• Paying interest on savings
• Local bank branches
• Making cash deposits
• Limited liability (a safeguard against loss)
• Watermarks on banknotes to prevent forgery.

Scots also help to set up the Bank of England and the Bank of France. These national banks, and many smaller, private banks, deal only with rich businesspeople and landowners. Later, in 1810, Scots minister John Duncan will found Britain's first savings bank for poor, ordinary people.

1698–1700

Disaster at Darien. Scotland's economy is depressed after years of war and famine. And European nations – including England – have passed laws to protect their own trade and keep out foreign ships and merchants. But there are many enterprising Scots who are keen to work hard and make money. They buy shares in a new overseas venture, the Company of Scotland. Its aim: to set up a trading colony in Darien, Central America (now part of Panama) – and to build a canal linking the Pacific and Atlantic Oceans.

Three thousand settlers sail – straight into disaster! Darien is like nothing they've seen before: extremely hot, steamy, rugged (no land to grow food), infested with disease-carrying mosquitoes, and without enough water. They've brought warm woollen clothes and smart wigs (as worn by rich, fashionable people in Scotland), but there's nowhere to shelter from the torrential rains or burning sun. Hostile Spanish ships patrol the coast and stop food supplies reaching them. Most of the settlers die, and investors in the Company – some of Scotland's most important people – lose all their money.

Scots in South America

In 1701, pirate Captain Kidd, a Scot who preyed on Caribbean shipping, is hanged in London. Rumours say that he has left fabulous treasure buried on a secret island.

In 1704, Alexander Selkirk is marooned (left alone as a punishment) for four years on the island of Más a Tierra, off Chile. His story inspires English journalist Daniel Defoe to write *Robinson Crusoe*, published in 1719.

1702

Small molehill, mighty consequences! King William dies in a riding accident – his horse trips over a molehill. He has ruled alone for several years, ever since Queen Mary died from smallpox in 1694, aged only 32. Now Mary's younger sister, Anne, becomes Queen of Scotland and England. She is the last Stewart ruler. A tragic figure, Anne endures at least 18 pregnancies but none of her children live long. If, as seems likely, she dies without an heir, who will rule? The English Parliament nominates Anne's cousin, the Electress (Princess) of Hanover in Germany, to rule England and Scotland.

Alexander Selkirk

The real Robinson Crusoe

Steps to Union

It is during Queen Anne's reign that the kingdoms of England and Scotland – which have shared the same monarchs since 1603 – are finally united. But the process is not at all straightforward...

1702
The Scots are not happy with the English Parliament's choice for Queen Anne's successor. No-one has consulted them!

1704
The Scottish Parliament passes the Act of Security: Scotland will choose its own successor to Queen Anne – it could be any Protestant member of the Stewart royal family.

1705
The English Parliament is furious. It passes the Alien Act. All Scots are now 'foreigners', and Scottish trade with England and its colonies is banned. This will bring economic ruin to Scotland – fast.

The Scots retaliate. An English ship, the *Worcester*, is captured in Scottish waters and its crew are accused of piracy. The accusation is untrue, but the *Worcester*'s captain and two crewmen are hanged all the same.

1706

Scots know that they cannot survive for long without trading with England, or without access to English ports and colonies all round the world. They must work with – rather than fight against – richer, stronger England. They must also accept decisions – even the choice of ruler – made by the English Parliament in London.

Seeing the Scots' problems, English politicians get busy and negotiate with top Scottish people. The English want Scottish land – and Scottish obedience. They also fear a combined attack from Scotland and France. They offer money, titles, jobs, and freedom for Scottish trade, if Scotland will join England. Discussions drag on for months, while Scots argue about independence. Printers rush out 500 passionate pamphlets, all giving different points of view!

1707

The last Scottish Parliament for almost 300 years meets in Edinburgh. It votes to join Scotland to England in a new United Kingdom. Scotland will keep its own Church, schools and laws, and some Scots MPs will join the English Parliament in London – but there will only be 45 of them, compared with England's 521!

What they said about the Union

Queen Anne, 1707:

'I desire and expect from all my subjects of both nations that from henceforth they act with all respect and kindness to one another, so it may appear to all the world that they have hearts disposed to become one people.'

Scots poet Robert Burns, looking back about 100 years later:

'Bought and sold for English gold – what a parcel of rogues in a nation!'

Scottish school textbook, 250 years later (1957):

'The union of the Parliaments did not destroy Scotland.... We still think of ourselves as Scots first and Britons second. We know that we are in some mysterious way different from the English. We are still a nation...'

1714

Queen Anne dies, and Prince George of Hanover is proclaimed King George I of the United Kingdom. He is the son of Princess Sophia, Queen Anne's cousin. Sophia is now dead and George is her heir. He is a Protestant, as the Scottish Parliament wanted, but *not* a Stewart.

George is fair, fat, fortyish and foreign. He speaks no English, let alone Scots or Gaelic. He's accompanied everywhere by his very tall mistress (the English call her 'the Maypole') and his very stout sister ('the Elephant') – and has kept his wife in prison since 1694.

There are *57 people* with a better claim by birth to the Scottish throne, but they are all Catholic and therefore unacceptable to most Scots – and most English. Chief claimant is James Edward Stewart, son of the late, unlamented, James VII and II. The rebellious Jacobites call James Edward 'James VIII'; everyone else calls him 'the Old Pretender' – or 'Old Mr Misfortune'.

Jings! These Jacobites!

After Killicrankie (see page 70), the new UK government fears and suspects Scots Jacobites, and sends spies to report on them. Secret agents include novelist Daniel Defoe, famous for writing *Robinson Crusoe*. His task in the 1720s is not easy...

Confusingly, Jacobites may be:

- French, Irish or Spanish, as well as Scots. All are keen to fight against England.

- Unwilling. Some clansmen are forced to fight by their clan chiefs.

- Protesters – against new taxes raised by the UK Parliament in London.

- Scots and English Tories (traditionalists), suspicious of anything new.

- Protestants. Many Jacobites are Catholic, but others are not.

- Lowlanders. The Jacobite rebellion is not a war between different regions of Scotland; rebels are fighting for control of Scotland *and* England. Around a third of the Jacobite soldiers come from the Lowlands.

- Bandits and cattle-thieves. For them, war is just a chance for fresh crimes.

King George's supporters may be:

- Scottish chiefs. The Campbell clan leader, 'Red John of the Battles', is one of his army commanders.

- Scottish soldiers. Half of George's troops in Scotland are Scots.

- Scottish scouts. A new UK army regiment, the Black Watch, is formed in 1725 to patrol the Highlands and search for hidden Jacobite sympathisers and supporters.

And the Jacobites are *not* Scottish nationalists!

It is treason – punishable by death! – to be a Jacobite. But keen Jacobites have secret ways of making their feelings known. They:

- Wear a white rose or a white cockade in their hat.

- Drink toasts to the 'king over the water' (James Edward Stewart, in exile in Italy).

- Speak highly of 'the little gentleman in black velvet' (the mole that tripped up King William's horse).

1708

James Edward, the Old Pretender, plans an invasion from Spain. It's cancelled because of bad weather – and because he has measles.

1715

The Scottish Jacobite army gathers at Braemar, in the Highlands. James Edward is late, but eventually joins them.

Better late than never!

1716
Jacobite armies march south. They cause fear and panic, but are forced to retreat by King George's soldiers at Preston in north-west England, and at Sheriffmuir, near Stirling. James Edward goes home to Rome.

1719
Exiled Scots Jacobite nobles land in north-west Scotland. But while they quarrel over tactics, King George's army arrives and scatters them at the battle of Glen Shiel.

Back in Rome, James Edward has other things on his mind. Surrounded by scandal, he elopes with the 17-year-old daughter of the King of Poland.

1722
A 'Jacobite' plot to overthrow the new King George II is 'discovered' in London. In reality, it's probably planned by the British Prime Minister to discredit Jacobites in England.

1740–1744

The Jacobites have a new leader. He's James Edward's son, Charles Edward Stewart: 'Bonnie Prince Charlie' or the 'Young Pretender'. The French promise 10,000 troops to help him, but storms keep the French ships in port.

Charlie is an unlikely Scottish hero. He's half Polish, a quarter Italian, has been brought up in Rome, and speaks English with an Irish accent. (He had Irish priests as tutors.) He's brave and charming, but hopelessly inexperienced – and arrogant, foolish and selfish, as well.

1745

Charlie (aged only 23) lands on the west coast of Scotland. He has just seven men with him, as the French army is now busy fighting elsewhere. He is told by the local clan chief to go home. Dramatically, romantically, he replies, 'I am come home, sir'.

Highland 'guides' deliberately send King George II's army the wrong way so it gets lost. This gives the Jacobites time to snatch a surprise victory at Prestonpans, in south-east Scotland. The battle lasts just 15 minutes! Then, to the horror of King George's government, the Jacobites march south, into England. They conquer Carlisle, Manchester, Derby... until they are only 130 miles (210 km) from London!

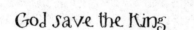

God save the King

It's autumn 1745, and the United Kingdom has a new National Anthem: 'God save the King'. It's not great poetry, but the fourth verse includes the words:

> May he sedition crush
> And like a torrent rush
> Rebellious Scots to crush;
> God save the king!

It is sung by panicking London crowds who fear for their lives as the Jacobite army advances southwards.

1746

By now, the Jacobites are running short of food, weapons and money. The further south they march, the less support they find. Prince Charlie is forced to lead his men back to Scotland. They wear out their shoes with walking – and demand replacements, at dagger-point, from the townsfolk of Dumfries. But they can't stay long in the Lowlands; it's too risky. So they head north to the Highlands and come face to face with King George's army at Culloden, near Inverness – in the last battle fought on British soil. The Jacobite army is cold, tired, hungry, outnumbered... and ultimately defeated. George II's army has twice as many men; its troops are better fed, better housed and better equipped, with muskets and cannon. Against all the laws of war, Jacobite survivors are brutally attacked on the orders of William 'the Butcher' Cumberland, King George's son. Any Highlander with a weapon is murdered; countless women are attacked. Captive Jacobites are executed, or sent abroad to UK colonies. Jacobite nobles lose their lands; poor, ordinary Jacobites see their homes burnt to the ground.

How sleep the brave who sink to rest, By all their country's wishes blest!

William Collins
(Scottish poet, 1721–1749)

Royal rebel on the run

Prince Charlie escapes, but spends months on the run. He drinks a bottle of brandy every day, gets lice and scurvy, and grows a long red beard. He escapes to the Outer Hebrides, then to Skye – thanks to Jacobite gentlewoman Flora MacDonald, who somehow disguises him as her maid 'Betty Burke', although he is very tall and very bony. At last, French ships arrive and carry Charlie away.

But Flora MacDonald's adventures continue. She emigrates to Carolina (now in the USA) – where she *opposes* American colonists fighting for independence from King George III!

Charles Edward Louis John Casimir Silvester Severino Maria STEWART
(Bonnie Prince Charlie)

- Born 31 January 1720, in Rome.
- His birth is announced to Jacobites in secret code – as a new Christmas carol!

  Adeste FIDELES, laeti triumphantes,
  Venite, venite in BETHLEHEM.
  Natum videte regem ANGELORUM...

  Oh come, all ye FAITHFUL, joyful and triumphant,
  Oh come ye, oh come ye, to BETHLEHEM.
  Come and behold him, born the king of ANGELS...

  [ye faithful = loyal Jacobites; Bethlehem = England;
  angels = Angles or Anglo-Saxons, i.e. the English]

- He is a noisy child and a troublesome teenager.
- At only 24, leads Jacobites in Scotland – and fails.
- At 26, flees to France in 1746, then Rome.
- Fails to persuade European rulers to back him.
- Leaves no surviving sons, but a dead baby girl, 'the Finsthwaite Princess', in England, and two more unofficial daughters.
- Bitter and disappointed, becomes an alcoholic.
- Beats his mistress; his wife runs away with a poet.
- Buried in St Peter's (Catholic) Church, Rome.
- King George III of England (perhaps glad to be rid of him) pays for his funeral monument.

Will ye no come back again?

Jacobite ideas inspired many later Scottish poets and writers, including Carolina Oliphant, Baroness Nairne (1776–1845), one of Scotland's great cultural heroines. From a noble Jacobite family, Lady Nairne worked in secret to preserve traditional Scottish poems and music, publishing them under a false name, 'Mrs Bogan of Bogan', so that no-one – not even her husband – would know. She also wrote new songs, often with Jacobite themes, setting her words to ancient Scottish melodies.

Here is the beginning of one of her most famous songs, about Bonnie Prince Charlie:

> Bonnie Chairlie's now awa',
> Safely ower the friendly main;
> Mony a heart will break in twa
> Should he ne'er come back again.

> *Chorus:*

> Will ye no come back again?
> Will ye no come back again?
> Better lo'ed ye canna be,
> Will ye no come back again?

[awa' = away; ower = across; main = ocean; mony = many; twa = two; ne'er = never; no = not; lo'ed = loved; canna = cannot]

CHAPTER THREE

NORTH BRITAIN

1746–1900

Clearly, the Jacobites can do no more. They must now get used to the Union with England, and their new Hanoverian kings. (There have been three so far, fathers and sons, all called George.)[1] For some Scots and many English, the rebellions have left suffering, mistrust, suspicion. Others feel that 'North Britain', as Scotland is now called, must be reborn, rebuilt and modernised.

---

1 *George I, ruled 1714–1727*
   George II, ruled 1727–1760
   George III, ruled 1760–1820

1746

The City of Glasgow holds a cake and wine party to celebrate the Jacobite defeat. 'Butcher' Cumberland is offered the freedom of the city, and many other honours. A new flower, 'sweet William', is named after him. Jacobites reply by naming a particularly unpleasant weed 'stinking Willy'.

Jacobite rebels, especially 'wild Highlanders', have seriously frightened the UK government in London. So Highland bagpipes, the Gaelic language, Highland dress and traditional Highland weapons are all banned, until 1785. Jacobite clan chiefs lose their lands and the power to maintain law and order among their clansmen. Many are exiled.

1747

Jacobite Lord Lovat is the last person in Britain to be beheaded. He has been captured hiding in a hollow tree, and says he's too old to mind about dying (he's 80). Fifty spectators are killed at his London execution when their wooden viewing platform collapses.

Hieland hame[1] or Hieland hovel?

Life for Highlanders is now very grim. In 1769, an English traveller reported:

'The houses...are shocking, formed of loose stones and covered with clods [earth]...or with heather, broom or branches of fir...The inhabitants live very poorly, on oatmeal, barley-cakes and potatoes; their drink [is] whisky sweetened with honey.

The men are thin, but strong; idle and lazy, except when employed in the chace [hunting]...The women are more industrious, spin their own husbands' clothes and get money by knitting stockings...The common women are in general most remarkably plain, and soon acquire an old look by being much exposed to the weather without hats.

1 Highland home

1750–1800
While Jacobites are being chased through the Highlands, Scotland's Lowland cities are being transformed...

Sited on the west coast of Scotland, beside a wide, sheltered river, the port-city of Glasgow is well placed for travel to America. Since the union with England in 1707, Glasgow merchants have been free to trade with English colonies there. They deal in the most valuable cargoes: tobacco and slaves. By 1775, 'Tobacco Lords' are importing around 20 million kilos of tobacco into Scotland every year. Other successful traders are transporting slaves from West Africa to work on American and Caribbean tobacco or sugar plantations.

These deadly trades are very profitable, and Glasgow's Tobacco Lords and their families live in fine style. They develop whole new streets, named after themselves or after colonies such as Virginia and Jamaica. They build splendid houses, filled with elegant furniture. As they stroll through 'Merchant City', the district they have created, ordinary people must make way for them.

Luxury... based
on human
misery

Scotland and slavery

- The first Scottish slave ships sailed between Africa and America round about 1650.

- In 1695, the Company of Scotland was set up to trade in slaves and slave-produced goods: sugar, cotton, rum and tobacco.

- Some of the first slaves were Scottish! Adult debtors or criminals might be forced to work as indentured (unfree) labourers to repay what they owed. Countless Scottish children were kidnapped – by Scots traders – to be sold as slaves. In the port of Aberdeen, boys and girls were locked in a barn until full shiploads were collected. Street musicians were paid to perform outside, to hide the children's cries for help.

- By around 1750, most slaves bought and sold by Scottish traders came from Africa. They were cheaper than Scottish slaves.

- Bunce Island, the main slave-trading port in Sierra Leone, was owned and run by a Scottish company. It sent over 12,500 African slaves across the Atlantic.

- By the 1780s, some Scots began to protest against slavery. City councils, university professors – and poets – called for abolition.

- Slavery was banned in Scotland – and elsewhere in the British Empire – in 1807.

Black Scots

Enterprising young men from many parts of Scotland head west, keen to make their fortunes. Many are employed as managers on Scots-owned plantations, marry African slaves and set them free. Some Scots settle in America, but others return home with pockets full of money. They build fine houses, and also give generously to good causes. Sad but true, some of Scotland's best-known schools and hospitals are paid for by former slave-managers.

More happily, returning Scots also bring their wives and children home with them. Around 1800, there are records of black children attending school in the city of Inverness and elsewhere.

An African at Culloden

In 2007, experts examining a tapestry picture of the Battle of Culloden (1746; see page 88) were surprised to notice the figure of an African man, surrounded by the mud and chaos of the bleak Highland moorland. Who was he? What was he doing? No-one has yet discovered his name, but he may have been a servant working for one of King George's officers.

1786

Scotland's most famous poet nearly emigrates! From a poor, humble family in south-west Scotland, Robert Burns has shown talent from a very young age. He writes in Scots, the language spoken by ordinary people, and has a remarkable gift for expressing deep thoughts and feelings in a direct and simple way. His works mock mean, narrow-minded, uncaring people – especially those in authority – and show sympathy for ordinary working men and women – and for slaves.

Burns is clever, witty, charming, moody, passionate, impulsive and, sometimes, irresponsible. He has failed at farming, and his love-life is in chaos. By 1786, Burns is in despair. He has no money, and his future seems hopeless. In spite of his belief in the brotherhood of all humankind, he plans to leave Scotland for Jamaica, to help run a sugar plantation worked by slaves. He is about to set sail when he hears the news that his first book of poems has become an overnight sensation in fashionable Edinburgh. He stays at home, dies young (from heart disease) – and becomes a national hero!

Love of women

This poem composed in 1794 is one of Burns's best-loved works:

O, my luve's like a red, red rose,
That's newly sprung in June;
O, my luve's like the melodie
That's sweetly played in tune.

As fair thou art, my bonnie lass,
So deep in luve am I;
And I will luve thee still, my dear,
Till a' the seas gang dry.

Brotherhood of man

On a visit to Dundee in 1792, Burns is said to have caught sight of a slave ship in the harbour. The plight of the slaves inspired 'The Slave's Lament', which begins:

It was in sweet Senegal that my foes
    did me enthral,
For the lands of Virginia, -ginia, O:
Torn from that lovely shore,
    and must never see it more;
And alas! I am weary, weary O:
Torn from that lovely shore,
    and must never see it more;
And alas! I am weary, weary O.

Robert Burns
(1759–1796)

Edinburgh Old Town: 'Auld Reekie'

By 1750, the narrow medieval streets and tall tenement blocks of Edinburgh are famous for smoke ('reek') from coal fires – and for squalor. Poor, homeless souls, sinister criminals and stinking heaps of rubbish all fester together in dark courtyards; the streets run with sewage as housemaids empty chamber pots from upper windows with a cheery cry of 'Gardy-loo!' (from the French 'Guardez-l'eau!' = 'Mind the water!'). Living arrangements reflect the need to keep above street level, if possible. Rich families occupy the topmost rooms, with respectable citizens on first and second floors and the poor down on the ground.

'What horrible alleys each side of the High Street... I ventured down one, and hastened back to escape from the spitting of two children who were leaning out of an upper window.'
Dorothy Wordsworth, English writer and traveller, 1822

'You might smoke bacon by hanging it out of the window!'
Robert Southey, English Poet Laureate, 1819

Edinburgh New Town: 'Athens of the North'

In 1766, architect James Craig wins a competition to design Edinburgh's new city centre. It's to be built in fine Classical style, copied from ancient Greek and Roman buildings. It's beautiful, but very cold. A bitter wind whistles through its open colonnades, more suitable for sunny, Mediterranean, Greek and Roman lands.

The citizens don't mind. They call their fine new city 'the Athens of the North'. It's home to some of the 18th-century Europe's greatest thinkers – and to the new *Encyclopaedia Britannica*, first published in 1778–1781.

'With regard to the buildings that have of late risen in this city with such incredible rapidity, we may venture to say that, in regularity and magnificence, they are scarcely equalled...by any in Europe.'
   Robert Heron, Scottish writer, around 1790

'Who indeed that has once seen Edinburgh, but must see it again in their dreams?'
   Charlotte Brontë, English novelist, 1850

edinburgh New Town: Athens of the North

Athens without the sun and heat, that is.

Stars of the Edinburgh 'enlightenment' include philosopher David Hume, economist Adam Smith, geologist David Hutton, mathematician David Gregory and chemist James Black. Together, they shape a new, scientific, way of understanding the world. Their teachings still have tremendous influence today.

The Strange Case of Deacon Brodie

In the daytime, William Brodie was a respectable Edinburgh carpenter and churchman – but he was leading a double life. At night he drank in slum taverns and partied with two mistresses. For all this, he needed money, so he stole from his wealthy clients – until he was caught. Brodie was hanged for theft in 1788, on Edinburgh's fine new gallows...which he himself designed!

Years later, in 1866, Edinburgh-born novelist Robert Louis Stevenson was inspired by Deacon Brodie's story to create his own amazing tale, *The Strange Case of Dr Jekyll and Mr Hyde*.

Medical matters

Edinburgh's medical centre is world-famous. Students throng to watch expert surgeons dissect bodies, to understand how humans are made and what causes disease. For their work, the surgeons need corpses, and there are not enough to go round. So they pay 'resurrection men' to remove dead bodies from churchyards – no questions asked. In 1829, a scandal rocks the splendid city of Edinburgh. Two Irishmen, Burke and Hare, decide that digging up bodies is too risky, and too much like hard work. So they trap Edinburgh's poor, needy and homeless – murder them, then sell them to doctors!

Meanwhile, in Glasgow, newspapers carry reports of a literally shocking experiment. This time, it's legal, but it's very disturbing:

In 1818, surgeons at Glasgow University are handed the body of an executed murderer. (Criminals' corpses are, by law, allowed to be dissected.) But, instead of cutting him up, they connect him to batteries to experiment with a newly discovered force: electricity! The dead man twitches and opens his eyes; he stands upright, his legs move... The audience of students screams in terror until, just to be on the safe side, the corpse is beheaded.

Hung,
electrocuted and
then beheaded!
Glasgow University
surgeons go in for
overkill.

Dundee: 'jute, jam and journalism'

- Around 1750, Dundee merchants import a new plant fibre – jute – from India. It's excellent for sacks, rope and carpets, but its rough, hairy fibres are difficult to handle. The answer: soothing, smoothing oil from whales caught by Dundee's fleet, the largest in Scotland.

- A traditional story tells how a Spanish ship carrying Seville oranges is wrecked off Dundee. Merchant James Keiller salvages the fruit, but his customers will not buy it. Keiller's wife, Janet, saves the day by turning it all into 'Dundee marmalade'.

- The story is charming – but it is not true! Dundee marmalade is first made in 1797 by James Keiller and his mother. Marmalade (as another name for jam) is already well known. But Dundee marmalade is new and different: it is made from bitter oranges, and contains chunks of orange peel. Together, both give it a special tangy flavour.

- *The Scots Magazine* (1739); *The People's Friend* (1869); 'Oor Wullie' (in the *Sunday Post*, 1936) and 'Dennis the Menace' (in the *Beano*, 1951) – all Scottish favourites; all created in Dundee.

Meanwhile, in the countryside...

1730s–1770s

Scotland's farming is changing. Landowners in the Lowlands are no longer content to rent their estates to poor farming families. Instead, they want to manage the land themselves, with the help of experts, often brought in from England. They want to sell farm produce, such as meat and wool, in bulk, south of the Border. There, English towns are growing fast. There are many mouths to feed, and many spinners and weavers to keep busy.

Cattle and sheep need few people to look after them, so country families can no longer find work as farm labourers. Nor can they grow enough food on their little plots of land – if they can still afford to rent them. Desperate young people, full of energy and hope, decide they must leave Scotland and seek their fortunes abroad.

Scots abroad

Foreigners quote an old French saying: 'Rats, lice and Scotsmen, you find them everywhere!'

Some Scots join European armies, from France to Russia. Others enlist in new British regiments being formed to defend British lands overseas. But mostly, they go to America.

Everywhere Scots settlers go, they take their language, music, religion, and usually the name of their home town or village with them. In the USA, there are 15 places called Aberdeen, for example. The name is also found in Canada, Australia, Antigua, Jamaica, Guyana, South Africa, Sierra Leone and Hong Kong. There is a Ben Nevis mountain in South Africa, and a whole province named Nova Scotia (New Scotland) in Canada. The map overleaf shows just a few examples.

- Scottish people, mostly young men, have been leaving Scotland to find work since before AD 1000.

- By 1600, there are Scots in France, the Netherlands, Russia, Poland, Scandinavia and Spain.

- The first mass movement of Scottish families is to northern Ireland, from 1609 to 1641.

- From 1621, Scots begin to settle in North America and, from 1698, in South America and the Caribbean.

- Between 1700 and 1800, over 60,000 Scottish people leave Scotland to seek a new and better life. Most go to North America. Others join the British army, or work for great Asia trading companies based in London. By 1800, one officer in three in the British Army in India is Scottish.

- Between 1800 and 1939, around two million Scots men, women and children emigrate, from the Lowlands as well as the Highlands. Some are forced out of their homes by landlords (see page 118); many choose to leave. They mostly go to the USA, Canada and Australia.

- Almost half the Scots who emigrate die young, from hardship, fighting, accidents or disease.

- Even today, more people leave Scotland than any other part of the UK. Around 1.2 million Scots live in England.

SCOTS

- Dunbar
- Fife
- Elgin
- Melrose
- Midlothian
- Fife
- Nova Scotia
- Glasgow
- Dumbarton
- Bannockburn
- { Aberdeen
- { Glasgow
- Strathmore
- Dunedin
- Munro
- Falkland Islands
- Dundee Island

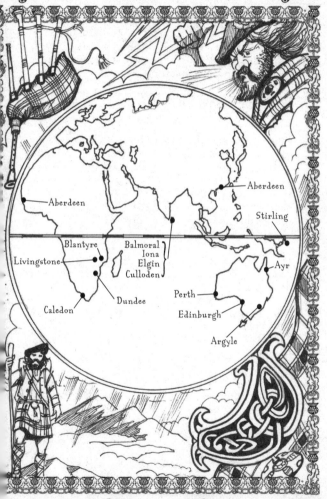

Aberdeen

Aberdeen

Stirling

Blantyre

Livingstone

Balmoral
Iona
Elgin
Culloden

Ayr

Perth

Caledon

Dundee

Edinburgh

Argyle

Great Scots! Scots overseas

John Stewart, Earl of Buchan (died c. 1430) Constable of France; commanded Scots army fighting for French king.

John Bonar (around 1483) Became a Christian saint in Poland.

James 'the Admirable' Crichton (1560–1585) Famous swordsman, poet, linguist and scholar in Renaissance Italy.

John Witherspoon (1723–1794) One of 11 Scots-Americans to sign the US Declaration of Independence (written by Scots-American Charles Thomson).

Samuel Greig (1735–1788) Founder of Russsian imperial navy, for Tsarina Catherine the Great.

John Paul Jones (1747–1792) Founded US Navy.

Thomas Blaikie (1750–1838) Garden designer to Empress Josephine of France.

Grace Elliott (1758–1823) Author of an eyewitness account of the French Revolution.

Lachlan MacQuarie (1761–1824) First Governor of New South Wales, Australia.

Alexander MacKenzie (1767–1820) Made first known crossing of North America.

Sir John Ross (1777–1856) Explored Canadian Arctic and located Magnetic North Pole. His nephew, **Sir James Ross** (1800–1862), discovered the world's most southerly volcanoes, in Antarctica.

Sir Gregor MacGregor (1786–1845) Led Venezuelan army – in full Highland dress! – and helped win independence from Spain.

Allan Pinkerton (1819–1884) Founded world's first private detective agency, in USA.

Daniel Home (1833–1886) Court magician to the Tsar of Russia.

Thomas Blake Glover (1838–1911) Helped modernise Japanese business and industry.

Mary Slessor (1848–1915) Medical missionary in Nigeria. Honoured as 'Great Mother' of her community.

Williamina Fleming (1857–1911) Pioneer astronomer, USA. Catalogued 10,351 stars.

Sir Reginald Johnston (1874–1938) Tutor to Pu Yi, the last emperor of China.

Mary Garden (1874–1967) Star opera singer in Paris, France, and Chicago, USA.

John Muir (1883–1914) Pioneer of environmental conservation; founded Yellowstone National Park, USA.

New Loyalties

Scots in America trade with and marry Native Americans. Some, like John Ross (1818–1866), who becomes principal chief of the Cherokee Nation, win fame and praise fighting against the United States government for the Native nations' survival.

Twisted traditions

Sad to say, but in 1905, the Reverend Thomas Dixon, an American of Scottish descent, founds a violent, racist organisation – and calls it the Ku Klux Klan. As the name suggests, Dixon intends that members should be loyal to each other, like traditional Scottish clansmen. He tells them to 'fight' for White supremacy using the sign of the fiery cross, the traditional Highland summons to battle.

Successful Scots

Many famous Americans have Scottish ancestry, from frontier hero Davy Crockett and outlaw Butch Cassidy to singers Dolly Parton and Elvis Presley. So do 14 United States Presidents!

Scotland's Robin Hood?

Other Scots turn to crime. Bandits rob wealthy homes and peaceful travellers – and ambush herds of cattle as they are driven from the Highlands each autumn to 'trysts' in Lowland towns. (In England, 'tryst' means a lovers' meeting, but in Scotland it's the name for a most unromantic market, where farmers, drovers, slaughtermen and butchers get drunk together and do business deals.)

The most famous bandit is Rob Roy ('Red Rob') MacGregor (1671–1734), of Loch Lomondside. Hero *and* villain, he plundered nobles' estates in support of the Jacobite cause, and gave cattle and goods he had stolen to the poor. But this famous Highland hero had a shameful secret: he was also a spy for King George's government in London!

1750s–1800s

'Sheep eat up men' – that's the Highland Clearances! Lowland-style sheep farming spreads to the Highlands, but the consequences are disastrous. Whole village populations are forcibly 'cleared' (driven from their homes) to make space for sheep and cattle. Since around 1700, the Highland population has grown rapidly, and there is no spare land for 'cleared' families to farm. Many communities face starvation. Urged on by hostile landlords, whole villages pack up their meagre belongings, clamber onto leaky ships, and set sail.

1800s–1840s

In Sutherland, where the Clearances are most brutal, houses are burned down with people still inside them, after families refuse to move from their traditional homelands. In 1816, one old man, unable to walk, crawls to hide in a disused mill. He has no food, and tries to survive by licking oatmeal dust from the floor. Only his faithful sheepdog stops the rats eating him alive. One horrified observer, Donald MacLeod, reports that this is 'as great a barbarity as earth ever witnessed'.

1805–1840

A new farm crop – seaweed! Highlanders who remain are pushed to live on barren, stony crofts (small patches of land). Life is a struggle. They dig peat or burn cow-dung for fuel, gather and sell seaweed (used to make industrial chemicals), and try to grow potatoes (which provide four times as much food value as grain). Some work part-time as servants or labourers for rich landowners, or as ghillies (men who help with hunting, shooting and fishing).

Others go fishing or gathering shellfish. But going to sea can be very dangerous:

1832

'The Bad Day': Thirty-one fishing boats are lost in a single storm off Shetland; 105 men are drowned.

1846

Another disaster: the potato crop fails because of blight, a plant disease that spreads rapidly in wet weather. There is famine in many country districts. Even more country Scots now emigrate or move to Scotland's fast-growing cities.

1846

From famine to fashion! A few well-meaning landowners try to find work to help hungry crofters. On the isle of Harris, for example, in 1846, Lady Dunmore sets up a new weaving industry in crofters' cottages, to produce Harris tweed. It becomes very popular, especially among rich English and foreigners visiting Scotland. Harris tweed is still used by top designers today.

1850s–1880s

And it's war! Many crofters are now having to battle for their rights. Deliberately, landlords refuse to rent them enough land to support a family. By the 1880s, many crofters are exhausted and half-starved. They stage rent-strikes. On the isle of Skye, women fight at the 'Battle of the Braes' against policemen who have been sent to evict them. On the isle of Lewis, in the Deer Park Raid, crofters try to take back good farmland that has been set aside for deer-hunting. The British government sends investigators from London, and, in 1888, a new Act of Parliament gives crofters protection from unjust landlords – but not much good new farmland.

floating free – to pray!

Landlords and tenants also clash over ways of worshipping. Since 1843, when there was a major quarrel among Church of Scotland members, most crofters have belonged to the Free Church or small splinter groups that have broken away from it. As its name suggests, the Free Church stands no outside interference in the way it is run; it is independent and democratic. Some landlords see this as a threat, and ban Free Church buildings from their lands. Crofters in Strontian, in the far west Highlands, find a clever solution to this problem, by building a floating church on their local loch. Elsewhere, Free Church members worship – when the tide is out – on Highland and island beaches.

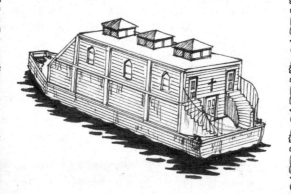

fascinated by funerals

Modern, go-ahead, 'enlightened' North Britain still has time to treasure some good old-fashioned eccentrics. In Edinburgh, Jamie Duff (died 1788) is famous for taking part in horse races – without a horse – and for his fascination with funerals.

Nicknamed 'baillie' (chief citizen) because of the home-made regalia that he wears – brass chain, hat and apron – he attends almost all the funerals in his city for forty years. Duff is so well known that some families pay him to be a mourner. But he is morbidly afraid of silver coins, and so his mother pays for a servant to accompany him, carrying a purse.

Baillie Duff is also famous for his devotion to his mother. When invited to share in a funeral feast, he makes sure to save a portion of food and a drink for her. He puts these in his pockets – without any wrapping!

CHAPTER FOUR

RICH MAN'S PLAYGROUND

ROMANTIC SCOTLAND

1750–1914

While country Scots are starving and being forced to emigrate, and city Scots are living in crowded, polluted tenements, a few rich, privileged Scots, together with English and European visitors, rediscover Scotland. Almost overnight, its rugged, rocky landscape turns – in their eyes – from 'bleak bog' to 'sublime wilderness'. Suddenly, traditional Highland culture is transformed from a dangerous Jacobite threat into something noble, picturesque and deeply romantic.

1776

Scots writer James MacPherson publishes *The Works of Ossian*. He claims that these poems come from an ancient Gaelic manuscript, and tell of Scottish and Irish warriors who lived long ago. Educated readers north and south of the Border are delighted. How wild! How fierce! How historic! Even French emperor Napoleon is said to take time off from conquering Europe to read them...

There's just one small problem – ancient Gaelic poetry was never written down. Are the Ossian poems completely fake? Or are they based on real Gaelic stories, passed on by word of mouth and mixed with MacPherson's own writings? No-one knows!

1792

The 17-year-old Jane Austen (later to become the world-famous writer of *Pride and Prejudice*) satirises the literary fashion for all things Scottish. In her short story 'Lesley Castle', her young Scottish heroine, Margaret Lesley, is writing to a friend:

'Matilda and I continue secluded from Mankind in our old and Mouldering Castle, which is situated two miles from Perth on a bold projecting Rock, and commands an extensive veiw[1] of the Town and its delightful Environs. But tho' retired from almost all the World, (for we visit no one but the M'Leods, The M'Kenzies, the M'Phersons, the M'Cartneys, the M'Donalds, the M'kinnons, the M'lellans, the M'kays, the Macbeths and the Macduffs) we are neither dull nor unhappy...'

1822

King George IV visits Scotland. His visit is stage-managed by top Scottish writer Sir Walter Scott. Sir Walter is determined to create a good impression of Scotland for the king – and for the world.

Sir Walter's image of Scotland is romantic, exciting – and extremely powerful. Like Ossian's poems, the vision of Scotland that he creates is part fact, part fantasy.

1 *The spelling is Jane's own.*

Tartan tomfoolery

Once in Scotland, King George agreed to wear a kilt – though, for modesty's sake, he added a pair of pale pink woollen tights underneath, in case a sudden gust of wind should reveal rather too much of the royal person. But the neat, tightly pleated skirt that he wore would have looked very strange to poor Highland men who wrapped themselves in rough chequered plaids in the years before Highland clothes were banned. Their kilts were just lengths of cloth, belted round the waist and draped over the shoulder. And they took them off for fighting! Soon, British army regiments and fashionable Scots are wearing tailored kilts like George's. A new Scottish garment has been created!

King George's kilt is made of a bright red tartan, especially made for his visit. It is called Royal Stewart. Until now, tartan patterns have mostly been linked to places, not clans, and have usually been made in dull, muted colours. But with the king's endorsement, a new 'tartan industry' appears, and weavers produce a dazzling range of tartans in vivid 'family' patterns.

From now on, tartan is used to decorate all kinds of objects, from ribbons to children's clothes, biscuit tins and tacky souvenirs. Other Britons – and people from abroad – search for family connections with Scotland, so that they may wear 'their' tartan. It makes them feel a little bit Highland, romantic and special...

ress to distress!
George IV cuts a dash
in his corset, 50-inch-
waist kilt – and pink tights.

1842

Queen Victoria and Prince Albert visit Scotland for the first time. They revel in the Scottish scenery, and come back every year until 1861, when Albert dies. In 1853, they purchase an estate at Balmoral, carefully choosing one of the least rainy valleys in the Highlands, and build a huge new castle. Inside, there is tartan everywhere.

While staying in Scotland, Victoria and Albert like to ride away to spend the night, in disguise, in small Highland hotels. Everyone knows who they are, but politely pretends that they are just ordinary English tourists.

Balmoral
Queen Victoria's Highland hideaway

After Albert's death, Victoria often retreats to Balmoral and seeks comfort in the company of her Highland servant, John Brown. Does she value his plain speaking? Has she fallen in love with romantic myths about noble Highlanders? There is gossip about their friendship...

When John Brown dies, in 1883, Queen Victoria seems heartbroken. She says, 'Byegone days were bright and happy... it seems to me that life is without light now.'

Royal author

Queen Victoria liked to sketch Highland views, and kept a diary of her Scottish visits. In 1868, she published *Leaves from the Journal of Our Life in the Highlands*. It became a best-seller, but not all readers agreed about it:

- British Prime Minister Benjamin Disraeli: 'A freshness and a fragrance...like the heather amid which it was written.'

- The Prince of Wales (Queen Victoria's son): 'Twaddle.'

1842–1914

Huntin', shootin' and fishin' are all the rage. Queen Victoria has set a fashion for summer holidays in Scotland. Rich Victorians, and visitors from Europe and the USA, rent or buy Scottish country estates, ideally with a castle. They spend six weeks in late summer there, entertaining their friends – and killing wild creatures for fun.

The expense is staggering. By the time they have paid for rent, upkeep, servants, ponies, guns, transport and lavish food for their guests, it costs estate owners £100 a day for each stag (male deer) that is shot, and £5 for each salmon fished from the river. In comparison, shoot beaters (helpers) earn 6 old pennies each day – 200 times *less* than the cost of a salmon.

The slaughter is immense. The Duke of Portland decorates his 'shooting lodge' in Caithness with the head of the thousandth stag he has shot. In 1871, Maharaja Duleep Singh, a friend of the royal family, sets a Scottish record by shooting 220 brace (pairs) of grouse in a single day.

Rich estate owners and their friends can afford all kinds of extravagant things, such as hothouses to grow pineapples and heated pools for keeping alligators, at Kinloch castle on the island of Rum. But sometimes their plans do not go smoothly...

In 1840, the owner of Brough House, in Shetland, builds a pretty summer house using stone from cottages pulled down during the Clearances. He stays there just one night: the building is haunted by voices of poor, homeless people.

Do it yourself

To dye the wool used to weave Harris Tweed, islanders use local herbs and lichens, mixed with plenty of liquid ammonia made from stale urine. On a visit to Scotland, Queen Victoria asks some wool-workers how they get the ammonia. Their tactful reply? 'We make it ourselves!'

Soap and drugs

What sort of person could afford a Scottish estate and castle? To take just one example, the island of Lewis, in the Outer Hebrides, was purchased from its Highland owners by Sir James Matheson in 1844, and then sold to Lord Lever in 1918. With fellow Scot William Jardine, who had made a fortune in the Chinese opium trade (and was mocked as 'McDruggy'), Matheson had set up a very successful Hong Kong trading company. Lever, from England, had become fabulously wealthy by making and selling soap. He fell in love with the Highlands on a holiday cruise in 1884 and had grand plans for 'his' island. They included roads, farms, woods, gardens and a whole new 'Mac Fisheries' industry, with a fleet of ships, an ice-house for storage – and spotter planes to hunt for herring.

But most of Lever's schemes were short-lived – and the local people resented them. After giving his castle and the whole main town on Lewis to the community, Lever left his island estates in 1923, having lost over £1.5 million.

Jardine

Matheson

CHAPTER fIVE

WORKSHOP Of THE WORLD

INDUSTRIAL SCOTLAND

1750–1900

I n the late 1700s, Scotland is a poor farming country, ruled by nobles whose land, wealth and titles have been inherited from past generations. By 1900, it has changed completely. It is the second most urbanised and industrialised country in the world, making goods that are exported everywhere – and the ships and railways to carry them. Traditional Scottish landowners are still powerful, but they have been joined by bankers, lawyers, factory owners, ship owners – and elected politicians.

1750

Coal, iron, water and workers – Scotland has all the raw materials needed for an Industrial Revolution. And, even more importantly, it has plenty of poor people. Men, women and children, 'cleared' from Highland and Lowland farms, are all desperate to earn money to pay for food and shelter. It is their work – just as much as the invention of new machines – that transforms Scotland into an industrial nation.

Industrial Revolution starts with a bang!

In 1759, the Carron Ironworks, near Falkirk, pioneers new smelting techniques to produce its deadly cannon – used by British hero Admiral Nelson to win the battle of Trafalgar in 1805. By that time, the Carron works is consuming as much coal (in the form of coke for its furnaces) as the whole city of Edinburgh. Carron make many other products, mostly for export. These range from iron cooking pots to portable steamboats cast in hundreds of separate sections. Each part is small enough to be carried by Scots explorers and missionaries – or, more likely, their native porters – as they trek across Africa and Asia.

Whole families work long hours in appalling conditions for low pay. Until 1799, some workers, such as coal miners, can be bought and sold by factory owners, like slaves or domestic animals.

A day in the life of a female mine-worker is pretty grim:

- Leave your youngest children with your grandmother or neighbour.
- Call your older daughters, and go to the coal-mine together.
- Hold a lighted candle in your teeth as you climb down a long, steep ladder into the mine.
- Grope along in the dark and dirt to find the miners. Two men will lift a huge basket full of coal onto your back.
- It weighs over 60 kilos, so heavy that you can hardly walk. But you must climb back up the ladder to carry the coal to the surface.
- Continue doing this for 10 hours every day. Often, you will weep with pain and exhaustion.

Until 1840, it's perfectly legal for you to work like this. Then, at last, underground work for women is banned.

Water, steam –
and child power

Machines that spin fine cotton thread using water power are the next innovation. Huge factories, known as mills, are built to house them. One of the largest, run by Robert Owen (1771–1858), is built at New Lanark, near Glasgow, beginning in 1785. Owen aims to treat his workers well, and provides schools and housing. But he still expects children to labour long hours in his mills – and has special lightweight machinery made for them to operate.

Technology is changing fast, and even the latest inventions soon become obsolete. From the 1800s, steam replaces water as the main source of power for spinning. By the late 19th century, Scottish cotton-spinning company Coats and Clarks is the fifth-largest business enterprise in the whole world! At first, this machine-spun thread is woven by hand, but from 1820, steam-powered looms take the jobs of skilled Scottish hand weavers.

Steam-powered machines all rely on an invention designed by Scottish engineer James Watt (1736–1819): the condenser. It makes steam engines much more efficient, and cheaper to run.

A load of hot air

That's the secret of Scots engineer James Neilson's hot-blast furnace, invented in 1828. It uses much less coke than previous furnaces to smelt iron, so Scottish iron goods become cheaper to produce. By 1860 there are 133 furnaces in central Scotland, producing over a quarter of all the UK's iron.

Gentle giant

The ultimate power tool for shaping iron, Scots-born James Nasmyth's steam hammer, first made in 1839, can also be used with great precision. Nasmyth has a trick to impress visitors. He uses his steam hammer to gently crack an egg, leaving its glass egg-cup undamaged, before making it deliver a full-force blow which shakes the building!

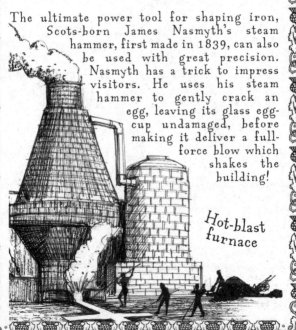

Hot-blast furnace

A clever idea? A new invention? It's probably Scottish!

Nineteenth-century Scots invent everything from grand pianos (John Broadwood) to bicycles (Kirkpatrick Macmillan), waterproof boots (the North British Rubber Co.), steel railway track (Robert Mushet), steam-powered tractors (R. W. Thomson), adhesive postage stamps (James Chalmers), vacuum flasks (James Dewar), ice-cream machines (William Cullen)… and much more.

The latest medical advances? Trust Scottish doctors!

Doctors in 19th-century Scottish hospitals and universities are making world-changing discoveries. These include chloroform anaesthetics (James Simpson), antiseptics (Joseph Lister), plastic surgery (James Syme) and the causes of scurvy (James Lind) and malaria (Patrick Manson). Scots set up the first mental hospital paid for from public funds, launch the first hospital ship, and – since Scots veterinary surgeons are very well trained – carry out the first scientific dissection of an elephant.

A struggling Scottish doctor, Arthur Conan Doyle, also creates the world's most famous fictional detective. Sherlock Holmes makes his first appearance in *A Study in Scarlet*, published in 1886.

Bubble, bubble...

No, not the witches from *Macbeth*, but the new chemical works at St Rollox, Glasgow. At the time the biggest in Britain – and maybe in the world – it's been built by Charles Tennant (1768–1838), famous for inventing bleaches and dyes used in new mass-produced cotton products. Many are made with processed urine, collected from Glasgow lodging houses.

Tennant is well-known for smelling the new mixtures he's experimenting with, to check on their progress. He uses some pretty dangerous chemicals – and they have disfigured his nose!

Scots ships take Scots soldiers and sailors all round the world

From the 1812 *Comet* (the world's first commercial passenger steamboat) to the mighty *Hood* (launched in 1914, and Britain's biggest-ever battleship), Scottish 'Clyde-built' vessels are admired worldwide. (Their name comes from the river that runs through Glasgow; it soon becomes a guarantee of top quality.) But, in spite of the skill and dedication of the men who make them, they are often built at a loss.

1869

The builders of the famous *Cutty Sark*, a masterpiece of ship design and manufacture, go bankrupt before she is even launched. The *Cutty Sark* is a sleek, beautiful clipper, designed to race with valuable cargoes – such as tea – from East Asia to Europe in 90 days or less. She carries an amazing 32,000 sq ft (2,972 sq m) of sail, and can travel at 17 knots (31.5 kph). Her strange name (it means 'short petticoat') comes from 'Tam o' Shanter', a poem by Robert Burns about a witch dancing in a graveyard (see opposite).

...And wow! Tam saw an unco sight!
Warlocks and witches in a dance...
They reel'd, they set, they cross'd, they cleekit,
Till ilka carlin swat and reekit,
And coost her duddies to the wark,
And linket at it in her sark!
...There was ae winsome wench and wawlie,
That night enlisted in the core...
Her cutty sark, o Paisely harn,
That while a lassie she had worn,
In longitude though sorely scanty
It was her best, and she was vauntie...

[...And wow! Tam saw a very strange sight!
Wizards and witches dancing together...
They danced reels with fancy steps, clasping
   each other tightly,
Until each old woman was sweaty and steaming,
And threw her rags off, to dance faster,
Skipping around wearing just her petticoat!
.... There was a very pretty young woman,
Who chose that night to join the group...
She wore a short petticoat of rough Paisley
   cloth.
It had been made for her when she was just
   a girl.
It was now shockingly short,
But it was her best, and she was proud of it...]

Today, Scots all round the world recite 'Tam
o' Shanter' on Burns Night, held every year on
25 January to celebrate Robert Burns's birth in
1759. Curiously, the first Burns suppers were
held on the 29th, because Burns's friends and
fans got his birthday wrong!

1840s–1880s

Railway mania comes to Scotland. The first Scottish railways – such as the Tranent and Cockenzie Waggonway, completed in 1722 – are made of wood. They are built for hauling coal from mines to ports on the coast. A hundred and fifty years later, royalty – and some Scots nobles – have their own private steam trains, and railway lines link all the distant regions of Scotland. In the years in between, there is 'railway mania' when competition to build new lines leads to great engineering triumphs – and disasters…

1878–1879

The Tay Bridge is opened by Queen Victoria, who travels across it on the first official train. Running for two miles across a bleak, windswept estuary, the Tay Bridge is the longest railway bridge in the world. But within a year, disaster strikes. The bridge collapses in a storm as a train is crossing. Possibly, riveted joints become loose, or perhaps cast-iron sections shatter. Seventy-five people are killed.

The worst poet in the world?

The tragedy at the Tay Bridge was mourned by
William McGonagall (1830–1902). Born in
Ireland, but living in Dundee, he was famous
for truly terrible poetry:

The Tay Bridge Disaster

Beautiful Railway Bridge of the Silv'ry Tay!
Alas! I am very sorry to say
That ninety lives have been taken away
On the last Sabbath day of 1879,
Which will be remember'd for a very long time.

'Twas about seven o'clock at night,
And the wind it blew with all its might,
And the rain came pouring down,
And the dark clouds seem'd to frown,
And the Demon of the air seem'd to say–
'I'll blow down the Bridge of Tay.'

...

So the train mov'd slowly along the Bridge
   of Tay,
Until it was about midway,
Then the central girders with a crash gave way,
And down went the train and passengers into
   the Tay!
The Storm Fiend did loudly bray,
Because ninety lives had been taken away,
On the last Sabbath day of 1879,
Which will be remember'd for a very long time.

1887–1890

The nearby Forth Bridge is deliberately over-engineered. For safety, it is made of 54,000 tonnes of steel, fastened with over 6 million rivets. It is much stronger than the Tay Bridge, but building it is a deadly task: 57 men are killed and 461 are seriously injured. Painting the bridge, to protect the metal from salt sea spray, is a continuous task. It uses 7,000 gallons (32,000 litres) of special red paint, and takes twenty men four years.

Working conditions are just as grim for labourers struggling to build railway tracks across a great Highland wilderness. Rannoch Moor is a bleak, icy, windswept plateau in the Western Highlands, surrounded by forbidding mountains. It is also an ancient wetland, hundreds of metres deep, made of spongy peat soaked with water. How can a railway be built across this bog? By floating it on rafts of brushwood! Countless men die – exhausted, chilled to the bone, lost in the dark or the snow, or sucked to their deaths in the quagmire – but at last the line is completed. It is still floating today; but even modern trains must travel across it slowly and gently.

1880s–1900

Hold your nose! It's the fish train! For thousands of years, travel has not been easy in Scotland. Until 1600, there were few wheeled vehicles; people – and cattle going to market – walked, waded or swam along tracks, through bogs and across fords. But now, railways bring the first mass tourists to Scotland. In 24 hours, you can travel from London to the Highlands!

Railways also create a new industry, based on the 'silver darlings'; shoals of plump, fresh herring that swim in Scottish coastal waters from spring until autumn. By around 1900, Scotland has over 30,000 fishery ships, based in ports all round the coast. Some ports are new and purpose-built. Wealthy landowners and government departments create new seaside settlements, such as Mallaig and Ullapool, in inhospitable places, simply to profit from the herring trade. Whole express trains loaded with fresh, dripping fish packed in ice leave Scottish ports for big cities in England. Gangs of 'fisher lassies' (aged from 16 to 60) travel round the coast, gutting and salting millions of fish as they come ashore.

New towns, new people

As Scottish industries grow, people move to cities to work in them. Glasgow is famous as 'the workshop of the empire'. It grows from 32,000 people in 1750, to over 750,000 in 1900 – a staggering increase of over 2,000 per cent.

Immigrants have been living in Scotland since 1171 – when Jewish residents are first recorded – and probably before. Now, many new city-dwellers come from outside Scotland. At first, most travel from Ireland, looking for work. By 1861, they make up nearly 7 per cent of the Scottish population.

From around 1880, Irish workers are joined by migrants from Lithuania, Italy and Poland. They work in factories, shops, cafes and mines. In ports, such as Dundee, Aberdeen and Glasgow, there are sailors and settlers from all round the world, from Russia to the Indian Subcontinent.

City living is bad for your health

Around 1820, a working man in Glasgow can expect to live for just 42 years, and a woman for 45. By the 1860s Glasgow is the most overcrowded city in Britain. Conditions in Scotland's other industrial cities, Edinburgh and Dundee, are also grim.

Scottish workers mostly live in tenements: apartment blocks three or four storeys high. Whole families crowd into one room. There are no kitchens or bathrooms, just a shared cold-water tap, and (if they are lucky) a communal toilet outside on the landing. In Glasgow, 20,000 people live in the old city market district. They have no drains. Conditions are no better in Dundee. By around 1850, there are only five indoor flushing lavatories for the whole city.

You can tell who's rich or poor just by looking – and not just from their clothes, or from cleanliness. By 1906, school inspectors find that 14-year-old boys from poor districts of Glasgow are, on average, 4 inches (10 cm) shorter than rich boys.

As late as the 1890s, one Glasgow baby in seven dies, usually from infectious diseases such as measles, scarlet fever and diphtheria, or from chest infections made worse by serious pollution. Charitable Scots set up 'fresh-air fortnight' countryside homes, where children can go for a short while to escape the smoke, soot, dust and dangerous chemical fumes that fill the air in big cities.

1800s

The Scottish diet develops. No, not deep-fried Mars bars or chips with cheese – those belong to the 20th century. And fresh wild or farmyard foods belong to long before 1800, when most Scots lived in the country.

In the 19th century, food for ordinary people in industrial cities has to be cheap, filling, high-calorie (factory work uses a lot of energy), long-lasting and easy to prepare. Most homes have no kitchen; just an iron range (fireplace) in the one room where the family lives, eats and sleeps. Meals are cooked in an iron pot over the fire, or else on a girdle (griddle) – a flat iron plate.

Porridge, made of oatmeal boiled in water, does just fine. Many families live on it. Oatcakes (oatmeal mixed with water and pressed flat) can be baked on the girdle. Scones or pancakes, cooked in the same way but made with white wheat flour, milk and eggs, are luxuries.

Boiled potatoes are the other great filling food. Cooked slowly over the fire, with onions or meat scraps, they make a meal called 'stovies'.

Stovies

You will need:

- 1–2 kg potatoes, scrubbed and chopped

- 3 or 4 onions, peeled and chopped

- 50 g shredded suet (beef fat), or dripping (fat left under and around roast meat), plus meat scraps if available.

- 50–100 ml water

- Salt and white pepper

Method:

1 Arrange the potatoes, onions, suet and meat scraps in layers in a big, heavy pot.

2 Sprinkle with salt, pepper and water.

3 Cover the pot and cook very gently for about an hour, or until the potatoes and onions are soft.

4 Stir occasionally. If the mixture is sticking, add a little more water.

For special occasions, try haggis! Although made with the cheapest, least appetising cuts, it's meat, and a treat. Haggis is the stomach of a sheep, cleaned and filled with its chopped liver, lungs and heart, plus suet, oatmeal, onions, salt and pepper. Other treats are potted heid (boiled cow's head, with the bones removed, pressed into a dish), black pudding (made with blood), white pudding (oatmeal, suet, onions) and tripe (cow's stomach).

> **'Oats: A grain, which in England is generally given to horses, but in Scotland supports the people.'**
> Dr Samuel Johnson
> (English writer, 1709–1784)

Scotland is one of the few places in the world where sausages are square, not cylindrical. Named 'Lorne sausage', (after a Scots music-hall comic, Tommy Lorne), they fit neatly between slices of bread for making sandwiches. Other fast foods, such as mutton pies and Forfar bridies (flat meat patties, sometimes including finely chopped onion), can be bought ready-made.

Slainte mhath! (Cheers!)

Drink becomes an industrial product, too. Rich Scots still drink French wine (thanks to the Auld Alliance – see Volume 1), but poor Scots drink beer. This is produced according to traditional local recipes of varying quality. It is said that men have to learn to survive their local brew; it 'would distemper (upset) a stranger body'.

Highland whisky, known since the 16th century as an almost-magical 'water of life', is also mass-produced for the first time. By 1900, 25 million gallons (112.5 million litres) are distilled each year. Most is exported; it is too expensive for ordinary Scots to drink.

'fechting fairs' or 'rational recreations' – which would you prefer?

So many people crowded together in Scotland's cities leads to social problems. City councils, political parties and religious organisations all encourage citizens to lead quiet, orderly lives. Instead of 'fechting fairs' (rough boxing matches, fought for money) and drunkenness, they promote 'rational recreations' such as pigeon-keeping, playing in a brass band, gardening, and making model railways.

Talk of the steamie

For Scottish housewives, keeping home and children clean is a full-time occupation. They hope, one day, to adorn their houses with simple luxuries, such as wally dugs (pairs of matching china dogs,) a waggety wa' (clock in a wooden wall-case, with a swinging pendulum) and a clootie rug (carpet made of fabric scraps).

Since few workers' houses have running water, housewives go to the 'steamie' – a communal wash-house with water heated by coal, and deep sinks for scrubbing laundry. Steamies are great places to meet other women and share gossip. Anything new or shocking becomes 'the talk of the steamie'!

Power to the people!

1816–1888

But what about the workers who dig the coal and smelt the iron and craft the ships and machines that make Scotland great? Slowly, their voices are becoming heard – and many of them are angry. They want political reform, higher wages and better working conditions. They join new trades unions, campaign to win the vote, and – inspired by revolts in France and Ireland – plan a revolution!

1816
In 1816, around 40,000 workers join a rally in Glasgow to demand a voice in government, and cheaper food for their families.

1820
Around 60,000 workers in west Scotland go on strike for a week. Groups march on Carron ironworks, hoping to seize weapons, but they are driven back by soldiers at the 'Battle of Bonnybridge', near Falkirk. Fifty of their leaders are tried for treason; nineteen are transported to Australia and another three are executed.

1832
Glasgow (now the biggest city in Scotland) gets its first-ever Member of Parliament.

ON STRIKE

1867

Male householders in towns, and men in better-class rented rooms, win the vote, but many poor working men will not be allowed to vote until 1918.

1888

Activist James Keir Hardie, a Scottish miner, founds the Scottish Parliamentary Labour Party. Its aims are to 'educate the people politically' and to elect national and local politicians who will:

- Abolish inherited privileges (especially the House of Lords)
- Nationalise Scotland's rich natural resources, such as coal
- Run railways, waterways and banks to benefit the people
- Provide free education for all.

Hardie does not succeed in all these aims, but workers continue to organise, and the Scottish Trades Union Congress, which gives a powerful voice to all Scottish labour unions, first meets in 1897.

TOWARDS TODAY

from 1900 to the 21st century

cotland is changing. For a while, the future looks grim. Scots are slaughtered in two terrible World Wars; old industries decay and Scotland slides into mass unemployment and poverty. But, at the end of the 20th century, devolution brings new excitement – and fresh challenges.

1901

Scotland's 'other national drink' appears: a sweet, fizzy, non-alcoholic liquid called 'Irn-Bru'. This secret blend of 32 ingredients contains a tiny proportion of a metallic compound, ammonium ferric citrate. At first marketed as a strength-promoting product, Irn-Bru is now said to outsell cola in Scotland.

1912

Who smears treacle on shop windows, and why? Scottish suffragettes – campaigners for votes for women. They smash windows, throw stones, ring bells, wreck sports venues and set fire to churches to make their voices heard. The treacle stops the smashed glass flying around and injuring them.

1914–1918

'Ladies from Hell.' Scots soldiers in kilts win a proud reputation in World War I. But Scotland loses more men in battles than any other country, as a proportion of the total population. Whole generations from villages and city neighbourhoods die side by side in a single day. The loss is so great that new recruiting rules are made. Men from one district cannot all join the same unit; that way, there is a better chance that some will survive – for a while. During the war, 500 Scottish army pipers are killed, playing to give courage to men as they march into battle.

In Flanders fields
the poppies blow
Between the crosses,
row on row...

One of the most moving poems of
World War I was written by John
McCrae (1872–1918), a Canadian
army doctor of Scottish heritage.

Scuttled Steel

At the end of the war, 74 German battleships
are captured by the British and sent to Scapa
Flow, a British naval base in the Orkneys.
There, on 21 June 1919, the German admiral
scuttles (sinks) 70 of them, to keep them out of
the hands of the British. It is the largest loss of
warships in one day at any time, anywhere –
and it all happens in front of the amazed eyes of
a party of visiting schoolchildren!

Years later, steel from these scuttled
battleships becomes a valuable resource for
Scotland. It is used in new high-tech medical
scanners (pioneered, of course, by Scots: Ian
Donald and John Mallard). Scuttled steel does
not contain radioactive particles which might
make scanners give false results, unlike steel
made after 1945, when the first nuclear
weapons were exploded, scattering radioactive
particles all round the world.

1919

Tanks in George Square, Glasgow! What are they doing? Chasing striking workers from Scottish shipyards who have occupied the centre of Glasgow. For years, working men have been protesting about cheap, unskilled people (women and boys) taking over their jobs, low pay, long hours, and machines that are replacing human workers.

Scotland has already sent the first two working-class Members to the UK Parliament in London (Keir Hardie and John Burns, both in 1892). Now, workers support left-wing political groups, especially the newly formed Labour Party, and even the Communists. Because of this, they are nicknamed 'Red Clydesiders'. The British government fears that they want a Communist revolution, like the one that shook Russia just two years ago.

1926

Scottish inventor John Logie Baird makes the first live, moving, black and white television transmission. Two years later, he shows that coloured TV is possible, also. To receive the TV signals, he constructs the world's first television set using a hatbox, some scissors, lenses from bicycle lights, a big wooden tea-chest, sealing wax and string!

Baird is clever and curious, and starts work on many other inventions. These include making diamonds from coal (his experiment blows up Glasgow's electricity supply), a glass shaving razor (it cracks), shoes with air-cushion soles (they go pop), and special insulating socks, which – perhaps surprisingly – do successfully keep feet warm.

1930s

Even though times are hard in the worldwide Great Depression, working-class Scots can still scrape together a few pennies for cheap seats at the 'talkies' (movies with sound). Glasgow has the largest number of cinemas per head of the population anywhere in the UK.

1938

Hail to the Queen! The biggest ship so far built in Scotland is launched: the fabulous Cunard transatlantic liner, *Queen Elizabeth*. At 83,673 tonnes and 300.94 metres long, she's the last word in grandeur, luxury, style and speed. But already Scotland's shipyards – the largest in the world in 1914 – are facing closure. It's too expensive, in manpower and materials, to go on building ships in Scotland.

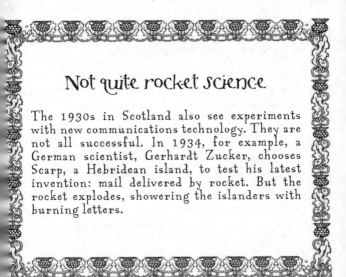

Not quite rocket science

The 1930s in Scotland also see experiments with new communications technology. They are not all successful. In 1934, for example, a German scientist, Gerhardt Zucker, chooses Scarp, a Hebridean island, to test his latest invention: mail delivered by rocket. But the rocket explodes, showering the islanders with burning letters.

Scotland at war 1939–1945

The nations of the world are at war. So is one brown bear...

- Scotland's engineering industry is back in full production, making weapons, ships and tanks.

- Scotland's ports house convoys of merchant vessels, ready to brave German U-boats (from *Unterseeboot*, German for 'submarine') to carry food and fuel from Canada and the USA.

- The 'Shetland Bus' (a secret shuttle service of fishing boats) ferries weapons and spies to German-occupied Scandinavia.

- Scottish harbours are defended by booms and mines. Lochs hide flying boats and midget submarines.

- Glasgow highways are stacked with giant gliders in kit form, ready to be assembled at airfields further south. Huge stocks of ammunition are hidden beside 'the bonnie, bonnie banks of Loch Lomond'.

- Young Scottish men join the armed forces. Scottish civilians endure bombing raids, blackouts, rationing, separation, fear, grief and loss.

All this is terrible, and normal for wartime...

...but wartime Scotland also has some surprises:

- Moors and mountains are used to train commando troops. The rough terrain and bitter weather make them tough.

- In remote Highland houses, secret agents learn how to be saboteurs and spies. It is rumoured that those who fail are kept prisoner, or worse. They know so much, they cannot be allowed to leave!

- Villages around the coast become Restricted Areas. Invaders might land there! No-one can enter or leave without permission – not even to go shopping, or meet their sweethearts.

- Scotland's population changes, as Polish troops, Italian prisoners, Jewish refugees and 'enemy aliens' arrive. The Poles bring a strange comrade: a huge, brown, beer-drinking bear. To enter Britain, it has to be given an official name (Voytek), army rank and number. After the war ends, Voytek stays in Scotland and lives peacefully until 1963 in Edinburgh Zoo.

- The Scottish island of Gruinard is used for a deadly germ-warfare experiment. It remains contaminated with anthrax until 1986, when 280 tonnes of disinfectant and 2,000 tonnes of seawater make it safe again.

1941

In 1941, crofters on Eriskay in the Outer Hebrides find treasure! They manage to save 24,000 cases of whisky from a shipwreck. The rescue inspires a famous film, *Whisky Galore* – but that tells only part of the story. (The islanders also found bundles of banknotes in the wreck, but didn't tell outsiders!)

Whisky Galore features stereotypes that offend many Scottish people. Since the 19th century, popular entertainers have portrayed Scots as dour,[1] grimly religious, mean, violent, fatalistic – or uncontrollably drunk and romantic. Some Scots entertainers, such as Harry Lauder (always clad in tartan from head to toe), have – alas – played up to these false images.

1952

Who's counting? The Scottish Nationalists, that's who! They strongly object to the royal cipher on the latest Royal Mail postboxes. It shows the initials of the UK's new queen, Elizabeth: EIIR. She is the second English queen of that name – but only the first to rule Scotland. Mysteriously, the postboxes vanish – for ever – from Scottish street corners.

1 *a Scots word meaning 'harsh and miserable'*

1950s–1970s

Scottish cities have been badly bombed in World War II. New buildings are urgently needed to replace shattered houses and old, crowded, dirty tenements. Whole new towns are built at East Kilbride, Glenrothes, Cumbernauld, Irvine and Livingston. Between 1945 and 1970, around 20 per cent of Scots people are moved to quickly built new homes, often in tall tower-blocks. These 'streets in the sky' are clean, with kitchens and bathrooms, but many residents miss their old, friendly communities. After 1979, many tower blocks are blown up. They have begun to leak and crumble, and are fast becoming slums.

Reasons to be cheerful

- In 1947, Edinburgh hosts a month-long party. Held every year since, the Edinburgh Festival is now the world's greatest arts celebration.

- In 1958, Christmas becomes a public holiday in Scotland. Since 1563, when it was banned by strict Protestants, Christmas has been a normal working day, and Scots celebrate New Year instead. Now they can enjoy both!

- In 1962, Scottish actor Sean Connery wows the world as the first – and many say the best – James Bond. Other Scots entertainers include loud little pop-star Lulu, comedian Billy Connolly, wonder-woman percussionist Dame Evelyn Glennie and bands The Proclaimers and, more recently, Franz Ferdinand.

- In 1967, the first Scottish Nationalist MP, Winnie Ewing, is elected to the UK Parliament in London. Most Scots don't want full independence, but are pleased to hear a forceful voice speaking up for Scotland.

- 'Glasgow's Miles Better!' This clever slogan (a pun on 'smiles') attracts millions of new visitors to Glasgow in 1983. So do the phenomenal 3,400 live events – almost ten per day – staged during Glasgow's year as European City of Culture in 1990.

Sporting Scots

Scots sportsmen are victorious! From past giants such as runner Eric Liddell (who inspired the movie *Chariots of Fire* – and would never race on the Sabbath) and racing driver Jackie Stewart to legendary footballers Kenny Dalgliesh and Jock Stein and today's world-class golfers Sam Torrance and Colin Montgomerie – all are winners. So are tennis ace and two-time wimbledon champion Andy Murray and six Olympic gold-medals cyclist Sir Chris Hoy. Not forgetting the five women – also Olympic gold winners – who won the so-called 'Scotsman of the Year' title in 2002 for their prowess at the peculiarly Scottish sport of curling.

Scottish football has some star players and a nerve-racking tendency to combine sheer brilliance with abject failure. But Scottish supporters – the Tartan Army – stay loyal, whatever happens.

'Some people think that football is a matter of life and death... I can assure them it is more important than that!'
Bill Shankly (1913–1981), player and manager

'We do have the greatest fans in the world but I've never yet seen a fan score a goal.'
Jock Stein (1922–1985), player and manager

1965–1969

Hidden treasures! Gas and oil are discovered under Scotland's seas. Scottish Nationalists are delighted, and claim that all the profits should go to Scotland. Scots joke that Scottish homes will soon have four taps in each kitchen: one for cold water, one for hot, one for whisky and one for oil – and all will be free! But oil taxes go to the UK government, and profits go to the multinational oil companies that run drilling and pumping operations. However, Scots oil city Aberdeen, closest to the offshore rigs, grows very prosperous, and some of the taxes are paid back to Scotland in UK government grants and subsidies.

1969

Tartan? Out of this world! Unites States astronaut Alan Bean, of Scottish descent, carries a small piece of MacBean tartan with him when he walks on the Moon. But it is *not* true, as some stories say, that he leaves the tartan there as a flag, to claim the Moon for Scotland!

Nuclear North

Now it's not just monsters like Nessie that lurk in Scotland's lochs. Polaris hunter-killer submarines are also stationed there, as part of the UK armed forces, from 1967 (but maybe, secretly, earlier). They are replaced by Trident submarines from 1994.

The subs carry nuclear weapons ready to defend Europe – or end the world in minutes! Close by, the Faslane Peace Camp, started in 1982, becomes one of the world's longest-lasting protests.

1984

Crime chimes! Since 1980, there has been bitter rivalry in Glasgow between gangs driving musical ice-cream vans. Can a cool summer treat really lead to so much hatred? No! It's rumoured that the ice-cream business is really a cover for much more serious crime. Jokes about 'ice-cream wars' turn to tragedy when six members of one seller's family die in a suspicious fire. Two men are imprisoned, but protest their innocence and are eventually freed 20 years later.

1993

From Steel City to Silicon Glen. The last great Scottish steel-making plant shuts, at Ravenscraig near Motherwell. At its peak, in the 1970s, it employed 13,000 people and made 3 million tonnes of steel every year.

New, high-tech industries come to Scotland. Workers – a majority of them now women – assemble computers and electronic equipment, and staff call centres. Customers like a Scottish accent on the phone; they think it's trustworthy.

1996

The world's first cloned animal, Dolly the sheep, is created in a Scottish research lab. A scientific breakthrough, or a step too far? Opinions are divided.

1997

Scotland says yes! There's a referendum, and Scottish voters choose devolution: Scotland will remain part of the UK, but its Parliament – suspended in 1706 – will start to meet again. When Parliament reassembles, in 1999, 37% of the elected members are women – the third-highest proportion in the world.

Who owns Scotland?

After the referendum, many Scots are excited. They feel independent, and free! But they forget that half the land in Scotland belongs to just 350 super-rich people or companies. Many are from outside Scotland. The largest landowner, with 1.6 million acres (650,000 hectares), is the Forestry Commission, a UK government department devoted to trees.

In 2005, the new Scottish Parliament changes the law: local communities can now buy the land they rent from absentee owners – if they can find the money!

2000

For the first time, Mohammed is one of the top 100 names for Scots boys. It's a sign that Scotland is becoming multicultural. Today's Scots may be descended from settlers who arrived 10,000 years ago, or from people who reached Scotland much more recently from Italy, Eastern Europe, Africa, East Asia and the Indian Subcontinent.

Whatever their heritage, Scots like to laugh at themselves. Popular comic characters, such as 'Rab. C Nesbitt', a drunken, workshy waster with a loving heart and sensitive soul (played by Gregor Fisher), or the doleful Minister 'Reverend I. M. Jolly' (created by the late Rikki Fulton), mock some typical Scottish attitudes. But Scots from all backgrounds can be offended by outsiders who call them 'Jock' or 'Hey Jimmy!', or who make jokes about Scottish stereotypes such as kilts, whisky, haggis – and, most of all, money. After all, it was a Scot who said:

'The man who dies rich dies disgraced.'

Andrew Carnegie (1835–1919), multi-millionaire industrialist who gave most of his fortune to charity

Pylons in the Highlands?
Or ribbons in the hills?

Until the 1960s, many homes in the Scottish
countryside did not have mains electricity.
What powers them up? 'The Hydro': energy
generated from Scotland's fast-flowing
mountain streams. Since the 1990s, power also
comes from controversial wind turbines.
Electricity is carried through the glens by long
cables strung from giant pylons. Some say that
these were foretold by a mysterious Scottish
wizard; around 1675, the Braham Seer
prophesied 'hills strewn with ribbons'.

Take-offs timed by the tide

Modern transport technology makes remote
Scottish regions more accessible. The shortest
scheduled flight in the world – barely 2
minutes long – links the neighbouring Orkney
islands of Westray and Papa Westray.

But Scottish air travel is not always easy. On
the Isle of Barra, the only flat ground for
landing and take-off is the beach. Planes have to
wait until the tide goes out before they can use
the runway.

2007

Almost 16 million tourists stay for 72 million nights in Scotland. About half come to walk and enjoy Scotland's magnificent scenery; a quarter visit museums, castles and heritage centres. They spend over £815 million each year, and provide jobs for one in ten Scottish working people.

2009

Haste Ye Back! The Scottish Executive plans a special welcome for Scots from all round the world. 'Homecoming Scotland' is a year–long festival celebrating Scottish culture and Scottish people. With luck, vistors will find that Scotland, like its history, is old and new, real and imaginary, wonderful – and peculiar!

But, Scots or not, please remember:

'The world is neither Scottish, English, nor Irish, neither French, Dutch, nor Chinese, but human.'

James Grant (1822–1887), founder (1853) of the National Association for the Vindication of Scottish Rights

2009

Glasgow-born Carol Ann Duffy becomes Britain's Poet Laureate. She's the first woman – and the first Scot – to be so honoured.

2014

Glasgow hosts the Commonwealth Games and Paralympic Games – the largest multi-sports event ever held in Scotland. The candy-coloured kilts sported by Team Scotland attract great ridicule. Never mind! Cheering crowds greet the world's top athletes, and a very good time is had by (almost) all.

2014

September. Referendum time. Will they or won't they? In a record-breaking turnout (over 80% of voters take part), independence campaigners lose by 45% to 55%. Scottish National Party Leader Alex Salmond resigns.

2017

After Britain votes to leave the European Union, a second Independence Referendum is proposed by the SNP. However, the poor result for the SNP in the 2017 General Election, and the success of Tory MPs in Scotland, is widely interpreted as an expression of the lack of appetite for another vote on independence.

Scots words and phrases
you might like tae ken

A

a'ee oo all equal, all the same.

agley astray

auld lang syne days long ago. *Should auld acquaintance be forgot, And auld lang syne?* (Burns)

awa absent. *Three can keep a secret if twa be awa.*

aye always *Yer mind's aye chasin' mice (wandering).*

aye yes; **och aye** yes indeed.

B

bairn child.

bannock flat cake, traditionally made of oatmeal. *Bannocks are better than nae bread.*

ben (or **ben the house**) the best room; **but and ben** two-roomed cottage.

besom badly behaved woman; **gallus besom** woman with attitude.

birl spin round. *Morag kept on blethering as she birled around the danceflair.*

blether talk nonsense.

bonnie good-looking.

bothy farmworkers' hut; **bothy ballads** songs sung by unmarried workers living in bothies.

brae hill. *By yon bonnie banks and by yon bonnie braes…*

braw beautiful, fine. *It's a braw, bricht, moonlit nicht the nicht!*

C

cairn heap of stones, marking a special place. *I'll add a stone to his cairn (praise his memory).*

canny careful; **Ca canny!** Be careful!

canty cheerful. *Where are the folk like the folk o' the West, Canty and couthy and kindly, the best?*

ceilidh (from Gaelic, pronounced 'KAY-lee') party with dancing, songs and stories.

clarty very dirty.

cleg biting fly.

close entrance to a tenement; **wally close** entrance decorated with ceramic tiles.

clype tell tales.

couthy cosy, comfortable.

cowp overturn; also, rubbish tip.

crabbit bad-tempered.

crack or **craic** amusing stories, chatter. *There was awfu' guid craic at the ceilidh.*

D

ding hit. *Ding doun the nests and the craws (crows) wull fly awa.*

dirl vibrate.

douce sweet and gentle.

dour hard, grim, miserable.

dram a small drink, usually whisky. *Ye'll tak a wee dram?*

dreich gloomy, damp, cold.

droukit extremely wet.

drouthy thirsty, dry.

E

een eyes.
eke also.

F

fash trouble, annoy *Och, dinna fash yersel!*
frae from.

G

gang go, walk. *The best-laid plans of mice and men gang aft agley. (Burns)*
gigot leg of mutton, roasted.
gin (pronounced with hard *g*) if.
girdle flat iron plate for cooking. *You're like a hen on a het (hot) girdle. (You're agitated.)*
girn grumble. *That bairn wis afey (awfully) girney.*
glaiket gormless, clueless.
greet cry. *Eh enjoyed a guid greet at the pictures.*

H

hen dear *Aire ye all right, hen?*
Hogmanay New Year's Eve, the most important Scottish public holiday.
hoots! well, well!
hurdies hips, thighs, bottom.

I

ilka every. *Ilka lassie loves her laddie.*

J

jings and crivens! gosh! my word!
jinkin' dodging.

K

keek look, pry.
ken know. *I wouldna ken him if I met him in my parritch (porridge)!*
kirk church (Protestant).
kist coffin; big wooden chest.

L

lad, laddie boy.
laird rich landowner, squire.
lassie girl.
loch lake.
lug ear.
lum chimney. *Lang may your lum reek (smoke)! (May you be prosperous!)*

M

makar poet.
man husband.
manse house for kirk minister; **son of the manse** well-educated, dutiful person.
mickle little. *Mony a mickle maks a muckle!*
mon man (familiar). *Whit're ye daein', mon? (How are you, mate?)*
muckle big.

N

nae no. *There's nae luck aboot the hoose!*
neb nose.
neep turnip, swede. Haggis is traditionally
  served with bashed (mashed) neeps and
  tatties.

O

orra odd, extra.
oxter armpit.

P

peely-wally pale, worn-out.
piece slice of bread, sandwich; **jeely piece**
  jam sandwich.
puddock frog; **heid puddock** big boss.

Q

quean girl. *I've ta'en a scunner to that quean!*

R

ramfeezled exhausted.

S

sassenach southerner; English.
scunner strong dislike.
shoogle shake.
skelp slap. *I'll gie ye a skelp o'er the lug!*
skirl shriek or sing shrilly. *The skirl of the pipes.*

snell cold, biting. *It's aye snell oot, the day!*
spurtle wooden stick to stir porridge with.
stoor dust.
stot bounce; **stotter** an expression of
  admiration for something very big: *Whit a
  stotter!*

T

tak eat. *Will ye no tak a wee scone wi yoor tea?*
tattie potato; **tattie bogle** scarecrow (**bogle**
  = goblin); **tattie howker** potato picker.
thole endure. *He maun (must) thole his weird
  (fate).*
thrapple throat. *Ma stammick (stomach) thinks
  ma thrapple's cut awthegither (altogether)!*
trachled or **fankled** weighed down; tangled.
twa two.

W

wabbit weak and tired.
wean child. *Weans maun creep (must crawl) ere
  they gang.*
wee small.
wheest breath. *Haud yer wheest! (Shut up!)*
wifie woman; **wee wifie** little old lady.

Y

yin or **ane** one. *The Big Yin (nickname of
Glasgow comedian Billy Connolly).*

Timeline of Scottish history
from the Stewarts to modern Scotland

1371–1390 Reign of Robert II, the first Stewart king.

1381 Scots defeat English at Otterburn.

1390–1406 Reign of depressed Robert III.

1398 The St Clair family of Orkney claim to have sailed to America.

1406–1437 Reign of captive king James I. He dies, murdered, in a sewer.

1413 Scotland's first university, St Andrews.

1437–1460 Reign of 'civilising' James II.

1457 First mention of golf in Scotland.

1469 Scotland gains Orkney and Shetland.

1460–1488 Reign of James III. He confronts powerful nobles, who murder him.

1488–1513 Reign of go-ahead James IV.

1494 James IV ends power of MacDonald 'Lords of the Isles'.

1503 Short-lived alliance between Scotland and England.

1507 First printing press in Scotland.

1513 English slaughter Scots at Flodden.

1513–1542 Reign of James V, 'the Gudeman'.

1542–1560 James's widow, French noble Mary of Guise, rules Scotland.

1542–1567 Reign of Mary Queen of Scots. She marries the dauphin (crown prince) of

France, is widowed, and returns to rule
Scotland in 1561.

1567 Mary Queen of Scots' husband is
murdered. She elopes with Bothwell, is
forced to abdicate and flees to England.

1567–1625 Reign of 'Wisest Fool' James VI.

1587 Mary Queen of Scots is executed by
Queen Elizabeth I of England.

1560 Scots Parliament votes to make
Scotland a Protestant nation.

1603 Union of Crowns: James VI becomes
James I of England.

1605 Gunpowder Plot in London targets
James I.

1608 Scots Protestants settle in Ireland.

1621 Scots settle in Nova Scotia, Canada.

1625–1649 Reign of unpopular Charles I.

1638 Scots Covenanters protest against
Charles's religious policies.

1642–1649 Civil War between Charles I and
Parliament in London, leading to Charles's
trial and execution.

1650 Parliament's army invades Scotland.

1651–1685 Reign (in Scotland) of Charles II.

1681–1685 'Killing Time': Covenanters
persecuted.

1685–1689 Reign of 'brave but silly' James
VII (= James II of England).

1688 'Glorious Revolution'. James VII exiled.

1689–1702 Reign of William and Mary.

1689 'Bonnie Dundee' leads Jacobite rebellion.

1692 Massacre at Glencoe.

1695 Bank of Scotland founded.

1698–1700 Darien disaster in Central America.

c.1700–1800 Thousands of Scots emigrate, mostly to North America.

1702–1714 Reign of tragic Queen Anne.

1707 Act of Union: Scotland joins England and Wales in a United Kingdom, with the same monarch and parliament.

1707–1800 Scots cities grow rich by trading, especially in tobacco, sugar and slaves.

1715 Jacobite rebellion led by Old Pretender.

1730s–1770s Lowland farming reorganised. Poor farm workers suffer.

1745–1746 Last Jacobite rebellion.

1750s–1820 Growth of science and learning in Edinburgh. New Town built there.

c.1750s–1850s Highland Clearances.

1759 Ironworks open at Carron; start of Industrial Revolution in Scotland.

1759–1796 Life of poet Robert Burns.

1778–1781 *Encyclopaedia Britannica* published.

c.1780–1900 Scots industrial cities grow fast.

1785 Co-operative pioneer Robert Owen builds New Lanark factory village.

c.1800–1900 Thousands of Scots emigrate to Canada, Australia and New Zealand.

1812 Steamship *Comet* launched; start of great Scottish shipbuilding industry.

1820 'Battle of Bonnybridge': Scottish workers demand political rights.

1846 Scottish potato famine.

1879 Tay Bridge disaster.

1880s Battles between crofters and landlords.

1880s–1920s Scots fishing industry grows.

1888 Keir Hardie founds Scots Labour Party.

1892 Scots are the first working-class MPs elected to UK Parliament.

1914–1918 Many Scots die in World War I.

1919 'Red Clydesiders' call for better wages and working conditions.

1926 James Logie Baird pioneers television.

1939–1945 Scotland suffers in World War II.

1947 First Edinburgh Festival.

1950s–1970s New Towns and tower blocks.

1960s Hydro-electricity powers remote homes.

1965–1969 North Sea oil and gas discovered.

1967 First Scottish Nationalist MP elected.

1980s–1990s Electronics and call centres replace heavy industry.

1996 Dolly the sheep cloned.

1997 Scots vote for devolution.

1999 Scottish Parliament meets again.

2014 Scots vote 'No' to independence.

2017 Donald Trump, whose mother Mary Anne was born in Scotland, becomes the 45th President of the United States.

2017 The SNP lose seats to the other parties in the General Election.

Index

INDEX

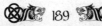